GIACOMO BRUNO

3X SPEED WRITING

How to write a 100-page book in 10 hours even if you start from scratch and have no time

I dedicate this book…to your book!

Title:

3X SPEED WRITING

Author:

Giacomo Bruno

Publisher:

Bruno Editore

Website

www.scritturaveloce.it

© Bruno Editore srl - All rights reserved by law. No part of this book may be reproduced by any means without the written permission of the Author and Editor. It is expressly forbidden to transmit this book to others, either in paper form or electronically, either for money or free of charge. The strategies reported in this book are the result of years of studies and specializations, so the achievement of the same personal or professional results is not guaranteed. The reader assumes full responsibility for his choices, aware of the risks associated with any form of investment. The book is exclusively for training purposes. The trademarks mentioned in the text belong to their respective owners

Summary

Preface by Alfio Bardolla — p. 5

Introduction — p. 7

Chapter 1: How to find your why — p. 11

Chapter 2: How to choose the winning topic — p. 51

Chapter 3: How to map the writing project — p. 96

Chapter 4: Copywriting techniques to write the text — p. 112

Chapter 5: 8+2 Specd Writing Techniques — p. 134

Conclusion — p. 157

Do you want to publish your book with Bruno Editore? — p. 172

Preface
By Alfio Bardolla

I have just achieved an extraordinary goal. I've been quoting my training company on the stock exchange for a few weeks and the magic is that it all started with a book.

When in 2006 I wrote my first book *Money Make Happiness* I would never have imagined such a success. Since then it has been translated and sold in the United States, South Africa, England, New Zealand and Australia. Then I wrote 5 other books, all bestsellers, and I sold over 300,000 copies.

But I want to talk to you about my first book. Because writing and publishing this text has made an amazing difference in my business. I went from being the one who "teaches things about money" to become the "highest authority on financial freedom".

Writing a book automatically makes you a recognized expert in that sector. And then becoming *Author* makes your authority grow immediately. You are no longer the one who has opinions, who teaches, but you are an Author of a book. And this made the biggest difference in the world for me.

Instead of going to tell a thousand things and explain what I teach, I'll give you my book, as if it were a business card. And this has a huge impact on your life, on the authority you have on your audience, on the business you have or that you will build over time.

We all have a book inside that we want to bring out, something that we want to transmit to others, and we would like to become more authoritative in our trade.

So who better than Giacomo Bruno to teach you to write a book, who better than the father of the ebook to make you a mastership in your area and an authority in the books world? I saw people who never thought about writing a book, being able to do it with Giacomo's instructions and automatically becoming the most requested people in that trade. Trust him in total peace of mind, because 3X Speed Writing and Numero1 ™ project represent a great investment that will return hundreds of times in your life.

Alfio Bardolla
Financial Coach No. 1 in Europe

Introduction

Write a 100-page book in 10 hours. It is a demanding challenge, but after writing 25 books and helping 600 authors publish one or more books with Bruno Editore, I can say that it is doable for everyone.

The numbers confirm this. A 100-page book is composed of approximately 15,000 words. If you commit yourself to writing 500 words a day, in 30 days you would have already written your book. But how many are 500 words? They are few. A simple medium-length email, like the ones we send every day to a friend. And if I add all the WhatsApp messages you send in a single day, I'm sure you would exceed this amount.

Let's think about it, with a minimum commitment of 10 minutes a day, in 30 days you would have already completed your book, without stress. It would be a dream, both for you that you wrote it, and for all the readers to whom your knowledge can change your life.

Yes, because writing a book means making a dream come true. And like you, I always looked for someone who believed in my dream, to publish a book to share my knowledge with other people. It was 2002 when I wrote my first book on seductive communication. I was proud of my work and I looked for a publisher. But I still didn't know which frustrations were waiting for me around the corner.

After doing some research and some calls, the best-known publishers made me realize that if you don't already have a name, there's no way. The lesser-known publishers, instead, proposed to me to publish with them, but in exchange I would have to renounce my copyright. Finally, the worst publishers asked me for 10,000 euros to publish, without offering any promotion.

This was the sad Italian reality. No one believed in my dream. But today I have to thank every one of them. Because I understood that the fault was not mine, nor of my book, but it was simply the situation of a whole sector like that of traditional publishing, which is dying. Crushed by ever higher costs, with less and less readers going to the bookstore to buy a book.

And if something similar even happened to you or you thought you've failed, know that it's normal and that it doesn't always depend on you. There are external causes against which you can't do anything. You just have to decide to take another way. I made the decision to self-publish my book in ebook format. A revolutionary choice at that time. And it wasn't simple at all.

I had so many fears. I had undertaken a new full project that I didn't know where it would take me, I had costs to face, a technology to learn, a job to create: *the ebook publisher*. No one had ever done it before, anywhere in the world.

I had a firm belief that with books you didn't earn much. And this thought turned out to be true. Apart from the millions copies of national and international stars, 99% of authors basically earn little or nothing. Statistically you don't get rich with books. I'll tell you this immediately, for intellectual honesty. Copyrights are a little percentage of sales, which is mostly eaten by bookshops and distribution, even online.

However, as a good engineer, I worked hard to find alternative solutions and I discovered that I could generate automatic income by bringing more customers to my other activities. So it's true, the earnings from copyrights are high, but the book can become the perfect vehicle to let you know.
Whether you are an entrepreneur, a professional or even an employee, a book gives you greater visibility, authority, competence. It gives you greater value on the market. And this can really lead to very interesting income.

But you have an enemy to fight: the distrust of other people. You can imagine how many enemies I have made myself in these 15 years. Especially at the beginning, every time I organized an ebooks conference to promote digital publishing, the big publishers and their related trade associations boycotted me and organized events in parallel at the same time . They were afraid of losing the bookshop and book market, so it was a real battle. Little David (me) against the great Goliath (all publishers).

Anyway, do you want to know something interesting? I never gave up the project I believed in. And that's the reason why I wrote 25 books and published 600 as an editor. To help, in Italy, 1,800,000 people with Bruno Editore books. To invoice over 10,000,000 euros in online book sales. And being one of the fastest growing Facebook profiles in Italy with over 1,000,000 fans.

Because nobody can tell you what you should or should not do.
No one can steal your dreams.
NEVER allow anyone to crush your idea. Because maybe you have a book that you dream of writing since you were a child and because of your experience, can change the life of many people. Never give up, also because...

... I can't wait to read your book!
  Giacomo Bruno
the father of the ebook

Chapter 1
How to find your why

In this book I want to be your coach: I will guide you step by step towards achieving your goal, writing your book.

I've been doing it for fifteen years, as an author and publisher. And with Numero1 ™ project I decided to teach everything I know to help you become a Bestseller Author. Why do I do this? Because like me, you believe in books too. And if you think about that, we're both crazy. I don't know if you know that, but in Italy 50% of people don't read a single book. Not even one. The other 50% read a book a year on average. And why are you here? To learn how to write a book that, according to statistics, will never be read.

But I will teach you the opposite, that is, how to write a book that will become a bestseller and will be read by thousands of people. Because the truth is that the ebook market and the digital publishing market are in huge growth. It's already been 6 years since digital has surpassed the book market. So you're in the right business, in the right place and even with the right person to guide you. We will have fun, because this text contains a real trail.

If you have my book in your hands right now, it's probably because you've met me online, maybe on Facebook, through some advertising. Maybe you've been following me since 2002, when I introduced ebooks for training in Italy. Or maybe you met me a few weeks ago.

This is also interesting, because the marketing of your book and the systems to publicize it are essential to succeed. If you want to write a book quickly, you must have a strong motivation. You must also know that all the work you are starting to do will not be done in vain: your book will end up in computers or on the desks of thousands of people, changing lives.

In fact today we can create authoritativeness from scratch, in a very short time, because the world has totally changed. Some time ago, to become authoritative, it took years and years of work. Applies to people as well as companies: years of work.

Today, within a year, you can build something big from scratch, whoever you are. And this is important. At the beginning I spent years to issue, but today, with the strategies that I will give you, improved in fifteen years of experience, your way will be much shorter. And I really promise you this.

I'll talk about the strategies to write a book quickly, but you'll notice that behind writing a book there is much more: there is a change of life, there's wanting something more, becoming authoritative, becoming the numbers one. It's not just about becoming number one on Amazon, but number one in general. Number one in life, for yourself, in your business.

SECRET n. 1: writing a book helps you become number one, not just on Amazon, but in life in general.

If you are an entrepreneur or a professional, writing a book can also be used for your business, to better promote your business, to make you more authoritative in your sector. This is the key word: Bestseller Author. Because being a bestseller author is something that you carry with you for a lifetime. You become once and it remains for a lifetime. Even beyond life.

My goal is to give you more than I promised you. Generally, companies, web pages, in training or in any other business, tend to promise too much and then not to keep their promises. In this case I want to do the opposite: I made a simple promise, teach you how to write a book, but here my goal is to give you much more. I want to help you change your life.

Bestseller Author, in fact, is an aim, a goal, but it is also an identity. Because to write your book you have to commit yourself. To write it in a certain way, you must follow the instructions. And I'll give you all.

But there is a concept of attitude that is really important: only the people who commit themselves will reach the goal.

Only people who will be punctual. It's not about being just on time to take maybe 10 minutes a day to spend working on your book, which is certainly important. But, in general, being on time is a sign of respect for yourself and for your time, as well as for the time of others.

Punctuality means following a logical thread. I will show you the steps, which are very simple. We'll do them together, you can't get lost, they're so simple that you'll try to make them more complex than they are. Follow the instructions I will give you in this book and everything will be ok.

Moreover, you must be present, here and now, while you read. Do you remember when you were a child? What were you doing? When my daughter does something, she only does that. She is totally intent in that activity, she has no distractions; if she's playing with the dolls and walking around, she doesn't notice anything because she's doing that. She's absolutely present to herself.

So, when you start writing your pages, you must have that same attitude. Leave out all the rest, leave the problems out, leave the distractions out, leave the phone and social networks out. Because the time to write the book that will change your life is the most precious time you have. The best invested ever.

If you are already an author or a writer, keep an open mind. Learn from scratch. Maybe you've already written a book, but here are new strategies. If you have written a novel, if you are not the author of training books and manuals, even in this case there is a lot to learn. So open your mind, again exactly like a child.

Open your mind on the exercises too. This book is practical and I will give you strategies to be implemented immediately. If you don't make the exercises, it's all useless. There are people who don't like doing the exercises or don't like to write on a sheet while they read.

I remember courses where even I didn't feel like doing the exercises. About ten years ago, I went with my wife to a course on the chakras. Do you know what the chakras are? The vital points from which the energy of the human body flows. I did not believe it so much, to the point that, when I received editorial proposals from someone who wanted to write books on the energy of the chakras, I rejected them all. When they convinced me to go to this course, I gave my ok, but I promised myself not to do exercises, not to be hypnotized by the guru on duty and not to do visualizations, meditations or strange things.

When I arrived in the classroom, I saw the participation contract and the release to sign to do the course. They asked me to sign that, if I had not done the exercises, I would have been expelled from the classroom. My wife and I looked at each other and we immediately thought about leaving, even if we had done 300 kilometers, because it was in a farmhouse near Bologna. But at the end we decided to stay, so, if we didn't like it, we would have left anyway.

The fact is that we are committed, we did it and it was a wonderful experience, where I learned, I lived and I discovered many things; a different way to manage my health beliefs and much more.

That course changed my life, so if I had not gone, if I were stuck on the exercises, I would have lost a great personal change. So, do all the exercises. And, in return, in the coming weeks you will have results that you can't even imagine.

Do you know the law of attraction? It says that if you ask the universe for something, it magically arrives in some way. I'm not completely convinced that it works like this. Indeed, I've discovered by my own experience that the real law of attraction is *gratitude*. You don't have to ask the universe, you must be grateful to the universe.

You must be grateful to the universe for what it will give you, for the opportunity that is giving you whatever you want, to your growth, to become more, to be more. Being grateful is something essential and it can change your life. Be grateful to have discovered the opportunity to become a writer and a Bestseller Author. Because it is true and, with a minimum of effort, you can turn it into reality in a few weeks.

And do you know what is the opposite of gratitude? To complain. Either you are grateful or complaining, this is the real evil of the modern world. Do you know someone out there who always complains? You don't do this, of course, and in fact you're in the right place at the right time. But when you hear people complaining, ignore them, so you stop them immediately. Don't come into the small groups of the whining who ruin the world.

The world fills us with bad news to command us, to show us everything in a negative perspective. Stop complaining, because complaining is something that comes back to you. If you complain, the others answer by complaining reflexively. If you only talk about negative things, it's a bit difficult to focus on positive things and goals.

Even in this book, you will like some things more than others. Maybe you'd like to get to the fast writing techniques right away, but you have to understand that, before writing, you have to mentally prepare yourself. Each step is not random, but it is a link in the chain that will take you to the result quickly. So you can't skip any step. Otherwise the block is around the corner. We need a strong "why", and in this chapter we will just start from here.

This attitude and these basic principles will allow you to emerge from a world that is totally in crisis. What are you talking about out there? Crisis is the key word. I'm not one of those who says that the crisis is a state of mind, which doesn't exist. The crisis is there, people are on the street, salaries are lower. This is the reality, but each of us can do something in his personal economy to get out of this crisis.

If we can't save the world, let's start saving each one of us. You can save yourself and maybe, with your book, you can share knowledge that will also help other people. Becoming an author allows you to get out of anonymity, because anonymity is the real problem.

Get out of anonymity. Who wants an anonymous husband? Who wants an ordinary woman? Who wants any employee? Who wants an ordinary item? Who wants an ordinary partner? No, no one wants "anyone". No one wants mediocrity. I want the special one, the only one, and you? What do you want from your partner? That is unique and that recognizes your uniqueness in you. Writing is one of those activities that makes you unique.

SECRET n. 2: writing a book makes you unique and allows you to get out of anonymity and personal or professional crisis situations.

In this book we will work to understand what is your uniqueness. But know that it's not your fault if today you don't feel unique yet or have not understood what is your uniqueness. It is that in these years the world has changed and keeping up with it is not easy.

The world runs, life runs and if we are locked, it's like if we were backing away. Instead, if you catch up, if you walk, start moving yourself and understand how the world works, you can go faster, specialize yourself, become unique. This is what we're going to do in these pages.

Let's think of famous people in training area. Do you know Anthony Robbins? He is the motivational trainer and number one coach in the world. How did you meet him? From a book. Or by word of mouth from someone who has read his book. It all started with a book.

Let's consider that: he wasn't born famous, he started with a book. He was an ordinary person, with talents to develop. Today Anthony Robbins is the number one in the world of training and personal growth. He has written several books, but the one I adore is *How to improve our mental, physical and financial status*, because it is the book that totally changed my life.

Let's think of other famous authors. Do you know Robert Kiyosaki, the author of *Rich dad, poor dad*? He is the biggest financial speaker in the world. He is no longer the real estate investor as a main activity; he was born from there, and in his books he talks about this, but it was the book that made him a star. He has sold millions of copies, the whole financial world knows him.

Reading this book, even a common person opens up new horizons on the business world. How to create financial freedom, how to create automatic income. Lighting concepts that can change the lives of millions of people.

Do you know Brian Tracy? He has written more than fifty books on success and on sale. *One million dollar habits* is one of the most famous. Sometimes he comes to Italy and takes courses on this. He's a great speaker and great writer. Bring out one or two books a year on business. Maybe your first book is not a bestseller, but the second one begins to be, with the third one you are famous, it becomes a necklace and sells thousands of books. All these people became famous after publishing a book.

Let's analyze Jack Canfield. He is a little less known, but he is the person who has sold the most books in the world. His book is called *Hot Soup for the soul*, maybe you've already read it. We're talking about 500 million copies sold. That is, almost 10% of the entire world population has bought and read this book. 500 million copies of a title is something incredible, it means being among the most read books in the world.

So, what is the concept? If you want to become authoritative, you must become an author. The same word says: Author…Authoritative.

SECRET n. 3: when you become author of a book, you become instantly authoritative and you are perceived as the most expert.

There is this conception, installed in our head, according to which if one has written a book it is authoritative. You know when people say, "He's famous, he's the author of that book about ..."? It is because the perception of authority is immediate. Then, it is clear that if you buy a book, you read it and it's bad, the author is burned. So our task will always be to write a high-level book.

This transforms you into number one. Number one in your niche, in your sector. If you write a specific niche book about how to use Facebook and its advertising, you automatically become an expert on Facebook Ads, because you have written a book on it. And when you present yourself to customers, you make a completely different figure than your competitors.

You are the one who wrote a book on that subject, you became the author Bestseller, you have sold thousands of copies. If an entrepreneur has to choose who to go to, he will choose you, because you are the most authoritative on the subject. An accountant is a professional like many, but if he specializes in something and writes a book on it, he becomes the only expert accountant of that something. So it applies to everyone, from professionals to entrepreneurs who want to revive a business.

By becoming number one, you can also do something for the world. What impact do you have on the world? How can you help people?

Because, you know, our books change people's lives. And this is often overlooked.

As a child you have a dream, you have a book in the drawer; then in the years it disappears, it is hindered, you forget it. But the dream remains to write a book, maybe to become famous, maybe to throw down your thoughts.

We forget that a training book, a manual of any kind, can change people's lives. Even a novel, a story or a poem can change people's lives, perhaps through a story in which to identify themselves.

SECRET n. 4: a book can really help people change their lives.

A manual that teaches you to have more self-esteem changes people's lives. Just as a manual that teaches you self defense can save your life. Because maybe that day you read about that technique thanks to which you then managed to escape from an attacker. So, give the right importance to the book in you.

Bruno Editore has helped 1,800,000 Italians to change their lives, improve their lives, in dozens of different niches. 1,800,000 people who have downloaded at least one book, a file, a PDF, from our site or from Amazon. They are a lot. In an Italy that does not read, they are really many.

When we first started, in 2002, ebooks were virtually unknown in Italy, but they had a slow growth also in the rest of the world. Up until 2007, we had 3% of the global ebook turnover. That is, the worldwide turnover was 30 million dollars and we had a million euros, in Italy, only ebook. Which is a crazy result.

What was the secret? I had chosen the training ebooks.

Still there were no devices to read novels, there were no ebook readers, the Kindle or even tablets. There was nothing. This feels like a thousand years ago. The training ebook worked right away because people, on computers, were looking for training and information, and then a book with a collection of ideas, thoughts and strategies could be read without problem.

It was a great success, but it took me years, and it was hard work starting from scratch. Indeed, from below zero. At that time I did not even have a PC.

The well-known monthly Millionaire, a few years ago, published an article about me, titled Editor of ebook, knew nothing about PC. And this is incredible, but behind it there is an extraordinary message, that is that you do not have to be a guru or an expert, you do not necessarily need a Master's degree or to have some kind of title.

It does not matter your past, where you come from or what level of education you have; you can always build something, you can and must write your book.

In 1997, when I was just twenty years old, I started the second year of Electronic Engineering and I had to do the computer science exam. But I do not have a computer. So I'm "forced" to buy it. And this is already incredible because, in 1997, twenty years ago, few were in possession of a computer; only the geeks had it.

I am obliged to buy the computer to learn a totally useless language like Pascal, but I enjoy it, I like it, in short, the entrepreneurial vein comes on me. I immediately connect to the Internet, with a 56k modem, do you remember? The difficulty of connecting, the noises ... The connection was very expensive, there were no providers yet. But after a month of browsing, I get fed up and start creating websites from scratch.

I did not know anything about programming, I started to download guides, in English, of html and I started to program some rather primitive websites. Compared to what was there, it was so, especially in Italy, where there were only 50,000 sites. Today there will be 50 million, maybe more. 50,000 sites: it was me and a few others.

Start making sites about my passions back then: video games, cell phones, ringtones. Did not you have a Nokia in those years? It was the strongest brand, destroyed by successive entrepreneurial choices.
These sites also start to earn me a little money, because I begin to discover how to be first on search engines. Over all. I was first on IOL, Altavista, Arianna, Yahoo. Yet there was no Google. Then comes Google and I'm first there too. Because it was easy. Put in the title of the page twice the keyword and you were first. So my pages were like this: "Nokia 3110 - Free ringtones for Nokia 3110". Boom, I was first.

Imagine how it would be today to promote your book by becoming first on Google for any word related to your topic. Would you like to go back in time and take advantage of this knowledge?

In the meantime, the years pass and, in 2002, my life changes completely. It was a normal day at the end of July when, on vacation in a friend's beach house, I found a book by Anthony Robbins: Notes from a friend. It is not very famous, it is a synthesis of the great tomes of Robbins.

I read this book at my friend's house and it enlightened me. My life changed. I understood that there is something more, that I was going in the wrong direction. For a series of personal and family reasons, at that moment, I was predisposed to change. Quoting a Buddhist saying: «When the student is ready, the teacher appears».

My teacher was Robbins' book, arrived by chance (or by attraction?) at that precise moment. I was predisposed, my life was changing. I asked my friend to lend me his book. I go back home, I read it again, I order all the books of Robbins and I read those too.

I fell in love with what I read, how to improve one's mental, physical and financial status, and I read it every day starting over again every time, all 500 pages, the same 500 pages for a month.

I apply everything I read, I do all the exercises. All. All views. I discover submodality, tracing, non-verbal communication, work on values, identity, limiting and empowering convictions.

And my life changes completely. An incredible job. I resume my life, I finish Engineering the following year and I graduate. Back in 2002, after that month, I said enough to all my websites. I'm no longer interested in business, ring tones or videogames. The Bruno Editore site is born: Autostima.net.

I register this domain and start writing everything I was learning from the application of the Robbins exercises. I put online free lessons on communication, self-esteem and motivation. I start writing, writing, writing. I had never even read a book.

At thirteen I had taken a course on fast reading. Which however had remained there. I had learned the techniques, but then I had never applied myself, nor had I ever read books. I started doing it at the time; the first year I read 700 books. 700 books in 365 days!

Fascinated by books, and passionate about training, I decide to start doing all the possible courses. My life changes completely, I start writing these lessons and these lessons then become a book.
My first book is called Seduzione (Bruno Editore, 2002), and it is about seduction, but more generally speaking about communication. Everything I had learned is in that book. There is really my story there, everything that I have lived in those years. It came out at that time and it was really incredible.

I never thought I would be the author of a book, for the shy person I was, for the young twenty-five that I was. I would have never thought of becoming a speaker, nor of being a professional trainer. I came to stand on the stage in front of 8,000 people. For me it was unthinkable.

I've never been an engineer, in fact my degree is hanging on a wall. But without that course of study I would not have bought my first PC in

1997, and maybe I would not have taken this path. I am of the idea that everything always makes sense.

Even the circumstances that can happen to you in life make sense and can give you direction. Maybe you notice it after a few years. For me, success did not come immediately. The recognition came after two years.
The first newspaper article about me, that of L'espresso, was published in 2004. So two years later.
I will not ask you to be patient for two years, because now I have learned the strategies, I will send them to you and, within 3/6 months at most, you will have already achieved your result: to write a bestseller book. Yes, it's all much faster now, because there are strategies and because you're really in the right place at the right time.

See what happened to me after fifteen years. Precisely because of my experience, my penultimate book, Marketing Training, has sold 23,000 copies in 24 hours. I would be curious to see if Harry Potter makes 23,000 copies in 24 hours, in Italy. It immediately became number one on Amazon, in the global ranking, not only in the marketing category, which in itself is very competitive, but it was the most downloaded book of Amazon. And now, for almost two years, it's still the bestseller number one in its class.

That book earned 150,000 euros within 90 days. How can one write a book and get 150,000 euros? It is the power of training marketing applied to books. And of all the fast writing techniques you will see in this text.

All this helping people, entrepreneurs and professionals to improve their business. So the money where do they come from? From having brought value to the market. Money comes when you help people. It is the recognition of the market. If your book does not help people, if it does not change and does not transform people, money does not come. No one is willing to pay to read your book, if it does not help them in something. But I know that inside you there is a great story to share.

Friends tell me that I am good at seeing the diamond in people, that is, in finding the positive aspects of an individual. It's a bit like the concept of gratitude, of not complaining and of seeing positive things. Here, if I know a person, I like to see his merits and even make them noticed.

Because often people are not seen and do not judge well or tend to be too bad with themselves, so they judge badly.

On Facebook is famous the image of the woman who is seen in the mirror more fat, but the man who sees everything macho, with the abs. Funny but true. Above all, women tend to judge more negatively than they really are, but even men often do not have enough self-esteem to see their merits, or because the world still tends to talk to you about your faults. People complain and you listen to these voices.

Instead, my role in this book is to show you the diamond in you. And your diamond is your book.

SECRET n. 5: your experience and your knowledge are a precious diamond that is hidden within you and must be freed.

Do you ever wonder what your talents can become a bestseller book? Here, I will help you discover this. I've been doing this for years with my books, with those of our authors, with the people I meet every day on social media.

You're in good hands. Because if on one side there is me, on the other there is the company Bruno Editore, the publishing house. You have seen the numbers, if I am the father of the ebook, she is the "mother" of the ebook. With 1,800,000 people helped, 10 million euros of online sales. It means that our books are sold because they help people. Yes, they help people, and this is primary.

And then because there is another important thing: the world is full of people doing marketing, and you will find many agencies - in the United States more than in Italy - that sell you editorial marketing, that is how to promote the book, and that they promise to promote you with publishers. But agencies only deal with marketing.

Then there is the publisher. The traditional publisher publishes you, prints you, takes you to the bookstore, but has no specific marketing skills. If you give the book to some Italian publishing house, also famous, it does not make you marketing, it does not promote you. He throws you into the bookstore, and you know how it ends? That 60% of the paper books remain unsold and ends up being pulped.

Do you want to do this? No? Then you need the marketing skills of the publishers' agencies and distribution channels.

Or it takes a publisher that knows how to do both, and therefore has the right channels, but also knows the marketing strategies. Here, this is Bruno Editore, this is us, and we are the only ones to bring together both aspects.

I often say that we are the Apple of publishing, because Apple has something special. Its uniqueness is that it produces both hardware and software. The software is perfect, optimized for the hardware, for the computer it is created to run on. Unlike Windows, which runs on a thousand different computers and crashes. So the secret is to dominate both channels.

SECRET n. 6: the secret is to dominate marketing strategies and at the same time have the right distribution channels.

But what are the right distribution channels today? The bookcases? Or search engines? Maybe it's Google? If I say that today we are in the new golden age, it is because it is really true.

Before I told you how 15/20 years ago it was easy to be first on all search engines, including Google. Unfortunately today it is very difficult to be first in the search results. And then there's another problem: what are people looking for on Google? The term "free" is still at the top of research. Those searching on Google for free information, in most cases, do not look for a product to buy.

On the contrary, there is another place, another engine where people try to buy instead. Amazon. Yes, Amazon. Who would not want to be first on Amazon? In the Amazon search engine there are 600 million credit card customers ready to buy your book, with One-Click technology. The books on Amazon are sold One-Click, with the data already entered. Amazon already knows my name, the details of my credit card and so on. Do I like the book? Click: I bought it. I do not have to re-enter all my data or the card details. It's already on my device, it's waiting for me.

This is a gold mine for you as an author. And today dominating the Amazon search engine is absolutely affordable for everyone. During my course Numero1 ™ (www.numero1.me) I dedicate a whole day to explaining how the Amazon algorithm works. It's crazy how easy it is, once you know the strategies.

For example, if you search for "marketing" on the Amazon Kindle Store, my book is first in the results for almost two years. You do not have to look for "formative marketing", just "marketing". One of the most competitive words in the world, because it is also in English, so it is really competitive with millions of results. They are on the front page. Because it's easy, and I know how it's done. I do not know how long this phase will last, probably a year or two more, so hurry up and write your book and publish it on Amazon.

I want to guide you step by step, give you simple strategies to apply, save you time. I do not want you to wait fifteen years to become first on Amazon.

I want to help you change your life as you write your book. And help change the world. With one person at a time, one author at a time, if we all get together, we can really make important numbers. Already a million and a half people are many, but if only you, along with the other thousands of people who are reading this book, write your own, let's reach many lives.

As Anthony Robbins has changed my life, I want to change the lives of as many people as possible. And I want to do it with respect and ethics. Why ethics? Because it is at the base of everything. We want to write books that change people's lives and in Bruno Editore we want ethical books, clean, made by competent authors and consistent with what they write.

So I do not want you to write a book about diet just because maybe the diet is a niche that has a nice economic return. Maybe you see that the diet sells well and, suddenly, you become a diet expert. Here, no, I do not want this. We must be consistent, in all things, so we will go to work on what you are expert on, your talents, your passions, what you like, on what others consider you expert.

We will do a great job and on that we will focus on writing your book. So monetization is essential, because clearly making an income is absolutely important, but money comes when there is ethics and when it brings real value to the market.

SECRET n. 7: Money is an economic recognition of the high value you have brought to the market with your book.

At this point I think you're realizing how much writing a book can really be a good opportunity. Maybe you already knew, or maybe it's the first time you hear all these concepts or this point of view.

People generally write a book for personal gratification, not for helping others. But, coming from the world of education, my attitude is precisely that of seeing the book as a tool for help and support. And I do not speak only of manuals, but also novels. Narrative can contain stories that can really penetrate people's subconscious and help them make a change.

So, if we have something to tell or share with others, it is really a shame not to complete a book just because we are blocked by limiting beliefs or strange ideas. When I talk to people during my classes, I often hear people say, "But I am not a writer." This is just one of many statements: "I'm not capable, I'm not an expert, the book is useless and you do not earn, the ebook does not work, I have no time, I have the writer's block, I can not write 200 pages" and so Street.

I would like to analyze these ideas one by one, because it is important to overcome them immediately. I want you to stay focused on writing your book quickly, and it's good that you get rid of limiting ideas like that right away.

«*I am not a writer*»

First of all, neither was I, so everything can change. Robert Kiyosaki, who we mentioned above, said: "I am not a good writer, nor a perfectionist, in fact I am not a *bestwriter*, but I am a *bestseller*". He said it because once, a client, during a course, had stopped him and told him that his book was badly written. Yes, in fact, he is not a good writer, but his book is selling.

It's important. One of Bruno Editore's philosophies, always, is not to find good writers to write, but *competent*. For us it is the most important peculiarity, because what is not particularly well written is settled, corrected; we have editors and proofreaders. If you have a valuable skill, it does not matter if you can not write. Pass it in some way and then settle it.

That your expertise can change people's lives. So we do not judge you if you mistake Italian or if you make a subjunctive, you correct everything, but we are interested in the effectiveness, that you are effective with the people who will read your book. We will take care of the shape. So even if you're not a writer, you can easily be a bestseller.

With this I do not mean that knowing how to write in Italian is not important, we would miss it. But I also say that if you give up your book because you do not feel up to it, it's not good. Your ideas are precious regardless of form and I want you to share them with the world. And if any professor of Italian is offended by what I'm telling you, maybe it's because he has too much ego. Form is important, but the contents have the power to change the world.

«*I am neither able nor expert*»

I want to tell you the story of Thomas Edison, the inventor of the light bulb. This is an incredible story. When Edison is six years old and attends the first grade, one day he comes home with a letter from his teacher. The mother opens the letter and starts crying. With tears in her eyes she says to her son: "Here it says that you are a genius, that you are so good that you can not stay at the level of your companions and that I must take care of your education, in a personal way". And he is all happy. So Mum, year after year, teaches the subjects, follows him, helps him, makes him understand things. An incredible story. Become the genius, the inventor, one of the most successful people in the world.

When he grows up, his mother dies. He, arranging things, finds the teacher's letter and opens it. Do you know what was written? "Dear Madam, your son is *retarded*, he can not be with his classmates anymore. You take care of his training because we do not want him here. Your son is stupid. "

That day the mother had not allowed those convictions to reach her son. The mother who was able to manage that circumstance changed a person's life. She saved her son's life. How many of us parents do, and remember to do it every day, even in small things? It's often not that easy. Really an incredible story.

So the idea that we are not capable or experienced is just an idea, it is only because we have not yet dug into ourselves, into our potential. It's only because we have not yet seen the diamond within us. I think you are an expert in something and that you are absolutely capable of finding all this.

«*The book is useless, you can't gain with it*»

I challenge anyone to say that he became a millionaire with the royalties of the books. If you have not written *Harry Potter* or if you are not Dan Brown, you do not make millions with books. In reality, the profit is given by the marketing system and all the related products behind the book.

The book, however, also has another value, which is that of authoritativeness, of the exit from anonymity. The book today is your business card. The traditional one, in most cases, ends up in the trash, because the people you give it to remember you for a couple of days and then, after a week, if you have not hit, they throw it away. But for the book it's different.

A book would never end up in the trash. The book remains in the library, maybe someone else sees it and a word of mouth is created. Maybe a film producer discovers your book and gets in touch with you. It happened to me: a book brought me so much fame that I was called, many years ago, to play in the documentary film *The Secret of the Web*. You never know where life can bring you.

SECRET n. 8: the book is the most powerful and effective of business cards and creates an immediate authority over others.

Also applies to an ebook. If someone sends me an ebook, I do not throw it away; why should I do it? I keep all the e-books. I put them on my iPad and on my Kindle. When I need them, I read them, they stay there, it does not cost me anything, I do not throw anything away. So the book is primarily authoritative, brand and positioning, to get what you want later: build your business, emerge, become the number one in a sector. This is what matters, not the focus on royalty, because royalties are generally very small compared to what you can build thanks to the book itself.

«Ebooks do not work»
Jeff Bezos, president of Amazon, in 2011 said: "Customers prefer ebooks to traditional books; I did not expect it to happen so soon. " By now, many years ago, on Amazon, ebook sales far exceeded those of paper books. And yet someone thinks that ebooks do not work. In Italy we are slow to perceive change. Even if it's never too late, this is a good year for you because you're a pioneer and you'll be among the first to dominate Amazon.

It is clear that a paper book occupies your readers' homes more consistently than the ebook and can therefore generate more word of mouth. But, as I always say to our authors, it is better to reach 2,000 people with an ebook than 50 with a paper book. You can give the ebook free of charge and without costs, both for you and for the reader. Instead, the book requires printing and shipping costs, and your readers a cover price; so a different economic commitment that certainly goes to decrease the numbers of people you can reach, especially if you start from scratch and you can not afford large investments in marketing. And my goal today is above all to help you create authoritativeness and reach as many people as possible.

"I have no time"
This is a classic. Who is it that has time? Every time you sell or propose something, or talk about opportunities, the classic objection is that people do not have time. And the answer is that for this you have to build a plan B, an extra income, an aqueduct of money, something that you build once and brings you money forever. The book is a classic example. You write it once, but it can bring you money forever.

I have products - books, videos, DVDs - that came out fifteen years ago, when I was really a child, and they keep straying. Because the topics of training, if it is not strictly technical training, will always be current. It is not that in ten years the concept of self-esteem will end once and for all. If you write a good book, following all the indications of the next chapters, the royalties will also go to your children.

«I have the writer's block»

The question is this: but the block, when you comment on Facebook or write on WhatsApp, you do not have it? You do not have it blocked when you need to send a fire email to the school because they've changed your teacher to your kids and you're angry? Or when you have a business problem and maybe the supplier is not delivering you the video you really need at that time? In those cases I could write a thousand words in a minute. A nice piece of book ready.

We write a lot of words every day. How many WhatsApp messages have you already sent this morning? Update your status on Facebook, reply to two emails ... and you'd already have ten pages ready, do you understand? There is no writer's block, it is a mental invention of those who are not motivated. Then I will explain the techniques to write quickly and overcome all this, but now reasons on the numbers. Between emails and messages we write the correspondent of 3/5 pages a day. Think about putting them to good use in your book. Instead of connecting to Facebook, write a few pages of the book that will change your life.

«I can not write 200 pages».

Write 100, then. Who says it must be 200 pages? In fact, my best-selling books are 100 pages. Ten years ago we created a format called ebooket ™, a mini ebook pocket. Faster realization, faster concepts, the essence of a topic. You can go to specific niches, where writing 200 pages would not be useful. Instead, those 100 pages of concentrated information are more useful for the reader, particularly suited to the ebook format and read quickly. People do not have time, and providing a book that you can read in an hour is much more comfortable for everyone. Work on 100 pages, your goal is 100 pages in 10 hours total.

I know that if you've already written books, some tips may seem trivial, but they are simply the result of experience. In these pages, I want you to learn from scratch, as if it were your first time. Learn as a child.

I am one who continues to learn everyday in life. I read at least one book a day, I attend training courses, in Italy and in the United States, I also go to those of my Italian colleagues. I am one of the few to do it, because I do not have a huge ego. Many colleagues instead would feel humiliated to participate in the course of another Italian.

I do not have time for the ego. I have recognition and gratitude for all the Italians who have helped me and from whom I have learned something, and this is the attitude that I would like to take forward too.

Not by chance, in the previous edition of the Numero1 ™ course, I had among the guests great names of Italian training experts, such as Alfio Bardolla, Roberto Re, Max Formisano. Because there is always a relationship of mutual respect and recognition. And maybe one day I will have Anthony Robbins as a guest, whose books have changed my life.

In this regard, I would like you to think of a book that you would recommend to a friend, a book that has changed your life. The last book, the one that has changed your life for the last ten years. One of those books that changed an entire sector of your life, from personal growth to professional growth.

What is this book? Write it here:

_____

Would you like to have you written this book? Would you like to be the author? Would you like to change people's lives? Why?

Responding to these questions, you will have realized that the first goal should be just to change people's lives. For me it is fundamental, probably because I experienced it in person and because, finding myself in a particular moment of my life, a book has changed my whole existence and my future.

Do you know the movie Sliding Doors? You arrive at a crossroads and your life is doubled. Maybe if I had not read that book that day, my life would have been in an office to be an engineer. Not that there's anything wrong, but I'm very happy with the choices I've made in the last fifteen years. But where do these choices come from? What are the reasons why it is important to write a book?

Many see in the book the possibility of earning money, royalties. We know that money has value, not money as an end in itself, but what you can do with money. Financial freedom is called this because it gives you more freedom.
So money = freedom.

Or write to become the number one in your industry. If you are a professional, an entrepreneur and you want to re-launch your business, being number one is important.

It is also true if you want to be the number one on a personal level, on the level of self-esteem, on the level of recognition. Think of all the people who never believed in you. They will change their minds the moment you become the number one in your industry and this thing will be official and objective, because you are the number one recognized on Amazon.
One reason can be precisely to challenge yourself and those who do not believe in you. Try to take it as a personal challenge, let's see if you are

really able to produce a book, to write it, to publish it, to earn money on it and to help people. This is the challenge, with you or with others.

SECRET n. 9: the reasons for writing a book range from personal gratification to professional recognition, from the creation of automatic income to helping others to change their lives.

One of the most powerful reasons for me is the willingness to not let one's own thoughts die. When I started writing my books, the great satisfaction was to have my own product, as if I had given birth to a child. Exit, is published, see the cover on Amazon and other libraries ... is like a child.

And you know that that child will live forever. He will never die. I will die and he will continue to live; that book will continue to be on the shelves, physical or digital. There are now 5 million books on Amazon. Who knows how many of those 5 million authors have already died. But books live forever.

Think of people like Napoleon Hill, author of Pensa and enrich yourself. Or Jim Rohn. Do you know him? He is the greatest motivational philosopher ever existed, the direct trainer of Anthony Robbins. He died a few years ago and it was a great loss, but his books continue to live, to teach people, to change people's lives.

Even your book will continue to do it, and more. I think, even as a son, that I would like to have the books of my parents. And I would like to have their books because, when I was twenty, I was able to ask them about things, but today they are gone, I would like to ask them more questions, I would like to know their thoughts when they were forty.

Bequeath your book, it is worth more than a property, more than an income. Leave your thoughts permanently written to help your children and anyone else. This also means giving value to life, yours, and not throwing away your knowledge. Wisdom comes as we get older, and then we die. Just when we are more experienced, we die. No, let's write it first!

Helping others is important. One of the first books I wrote is Speed Reading 3X (Bruno Editore), because it is among the first skills I acquired when I was thirteen. A friend of mine bought it to give it to her dyslexic daughter. The book was not created to help dyslexics, it talks about techniques to read quickly. But she used it for her dyslexic daughter, who had an incredible benefit.

He told me this: "My daughter has changed her life". He hugged me and I started crying. Because even I did not expect this result, it was not among those I had foreseen. But it had this effect. So you do not even know where your book can arrive, nor how it will be read and interpreted. You can really go beyond; together we can change the world, one life at a time.

But now it's your turn. As an exercise, I will let you write your why. You have to pick up the pen, the sheet of paper and write your own why. Why do you want to write a book? To make money, to help people, for gratification and recognition?

The reason, is always something important. So, asking you to write it in a few minutes is not easy. It requires reflection. It's something that you could even change as you write the book, or maybe, after you publish it, you'll get feedback like the one that came to me and, wow, you'll realize how much the contribution you can make to the world is important.

It is in progress, it can change. Nothing prevents you from continuing to expand it and write it down. What interests me is that it is a strong one. You must write a reason beyond all circumstances. Which of us has no circumstances? If we take a period of our lives, in the last 15/20 years, we all had a sea of problems. We had grief in the family, problems at work, maybe layoffs, money problems, difficulties in arriving at the end of the month. Who is it that did not have one or some of these problems?

So the circumstances are there and they are the same for everyone but, as Jim Rohn said, it's how you respond to the circumstances that make the difference. And that's where your is giving you support. If the reason is strong, you always get up again. If the reason is strong, overcome every challenge.

SECRET n. 10: if you have a strong why, there will be no conditions that can stop or slow down your way to become Bestseller Author.

If the reason is strong, when you have taken the commitment to write the book and the circumstances will arise - "well, that day happened to me that", "the washing machine broke", "my daughter is sick ... Come on, I'll send you to tomorrow "- nothing will stop you and you'll go ahead great.

Take the commitment to write your book every day for 10 minutes, carrying out 3 pages. Maybe you do not send that email, do not write that WhatsApp message, do not update your Facebook profile, but carry on those 3 pages of your book and then take care of the rest of your life. If the reason is strong, do it this way and in a month you will have completed your goal.

Find the true motivation that is inside of you. What is important for you, for your values, for your beliefs, for your identity. Find a strong reason to write your book, so that no circumstances can ever stop you.

WRITE HERE YOUR WHY:

_____
_____
_____
_____
_____
_____
_____
_____
_____
_____
_____
_____

SUMMARY OF CHAPTER 1:

- SECRET n. 1: writing a book helps you become number one, not just on Amazon, but in life in general.
- SECRET n. 2: writing a book makes you unique and allows you to get out of anonymity and personal or professional crisis situations.
- SECRET n. 3: when you become author of a book, you become instantly authoritative and you are perceived as more expert.
- SECRET n. 4: a book can really help people change their lives.
- SECRET n. 5: your experience and your knowledge are a precious diamond that is hidden within you and must be freed.
- SECRET n. 6: the secret is to dominate marketing strategies and at the same time have the right distribution channels.
- SECRET n. 7: Money is an economic recognition of the high value you have brought to the market with your book.
- SECRET n. 8: the book is the most powerful and effective of business cards and creates an immediate authority over others.
- SECRET n. 9: the reasons for writing a book range from personal gratification to professional recognition, from the creation of automatic income to helping others to change their lives.
- SECRET n. 10: if your because it is strong, there will be no circumstance that can stop or slow down your path to become Bestseller Author.

Chapter 2

How to choose the winning topic

In this chapter we will conceive the title of your book, which for me is the most creative and fascinating part. I love it so much that I personally take care of the titles not only of my books, but also of those of my authors, one by one. They have all passed by me.

I do not leave the title, which is the most important part of the book, to someone else. The editors can make me some proposals, but the last word, as editor, is mine. They study the key words and give me options. But the final phase remains mine, because I like it enormously and it is so significant that it must be worked out in the best possible way. Wronging the title means burning the book, so it's essential.

What is the path to get to a correct title? Everything starts from research and design. Search for what? First of all on yourself, understanding what your talent, your experience and starting the project from there. Only then can you continue with the writing of the actual book, but only when you have your project in hand, not before, otherwise here comes the writer's block.

If you sit at a desk and you have to write 100 pages starting from scratch, you block yourself. It would also happen to me. While if you have your project ready with all the details, the summary, the title and everything, there is no stopping you.

The research has several purposes, first of all to set the topic you are expert in. If you do not know it yet, you are an expert in something, and at this stage we are going to see what is your field of experience and then you can write your book. Just a few days ago a friend of mine was telling me that he would like to write a book but that he did not feel like anything. A small exchange on WhatsApp was enough to let him discover at least 3 good ideas. The day after he had already written 2,000 words!

Soon I will explain the advanced techniques, generally used by large companies, to work on your personal brand and to identify your reference and experience niche.
It's not the way people generally design a book. Many have an idea, they decide the title at random, just because they like it, and then they sit and write 100 pages. No, categorical, so it does not work. As I told you, I have an unconventional approach, which is why I will take you up very quickly.

Let's see now what are the steps; you will also have to do different exercises, because the research is above all inward.

The first question I ask you is this: what are you familiar with?

_____
_____
_____
_____
_____
_____
_____

I want you to write quickly, in 60 seconds at most, one or more things in which you are competent and particularly brilliant.

Second question: what are your hobbies? What do you like to do? What are your passions?

_____
_____
_____
_____

Third question: what results have you achieved in life?

_____
_____
_____
_____

Is there any area where you've had recognition? Are you good at playing soccer? Did you win a cup? Are you a good dancer? Are you good at doing something? It is not necessarily an official recognition, just a friend who calls you every day because for example you are the one good at managing the relationship with the partner. Anything that people see you as an expert, like a person who gets results. In private life or in work and in business.

The three answers are relevant because, if we mix them, we find points in common. There will be something in which you are an expert, that you are passionate about and in which you may have even achieved results, precisely because you particularly like it.

Are there any common points between these three areas? Reread what you wrote and see if there is a common thread, something that connects them.

Let's take an example. Maybe one of your results is that you had a fairytale wedding. Then you realize that, in fact, people always call you to ask for advice on this. Also you really like your wedding, you take time because it is essential for you. So an idea for a book could be just telling your experience showing how to make a wedding work. And it would be a bestseller.

Now, report the same reasoning to your field, to your sector, with the answers you gave before. Start collecting ideas about what you wrote and understand what your idea of book might be.

SECRET n. 11: Do a thorough inner research to understand what you are experienced, what you like to do and what results you have achieved in life.

Once this is done, I must tell you a secret. There is also a fourth question. And, if you want to make high numbers and become bestsellers, it's essential.

Fourth question: is it also a subject for which people are willing to pay? How is it "monetizable" (ie, capable of generating rents)? _____

_____

_____ _____

_____

_____

The marriage argument would certainly be; in Italy we have a huge audience that would be interested in better relationships. But would people instead pay to know a possible passion in snail breeding? Probably not. It is always better to stay in a slightly wider categories.

Compare this issue with what you wrote or thought, check if it is monetizable. Remember that someone must be willing to pay for the information you have to share.

Otherwise they have no market value. Not because they have no value in themselves, but because if the topic is not of interest you are not helping anyone.

Instead I want to bring you to become Bestseller Author, make you understand what are the potential of your book and which are the best-selling categories in Italy. Do you want to know? I know them very well, not because they read them on some American book, but because they are extracted from the publisher's database that has sold more ebooks in Italy: Bruno Editore.

Below you will find, in alphabetical order, the 20 categories that in Italy are mostly in the publishing field. Data in the hand:

- Learning
- Self esteem
- Companies
- Welfare bag
- Coaching
- Communication

- Economy
- Parents
- To gain
- Properties
- Computer technology
- Work
- Marketing
- NLP
- Psychology
- Relations
- Free time
- Sport
- Sale

These categories represent exactly 15 years of work and research that I have done for my publishing house. At the beginning we did not have categories, but a bunch of books, then slowly we started to divide them into categories and finally we saw which ones sold more and which less.

We cut the ones that sold less and we divided them according to those that sold the most; the ebooks that remained outside, we made sure to include them in these categories. Maybe we asked the author to modify it to make it more salable.

These are the 20 best-selling categories in Italy and are all 20 relevant. Hence, Italian data for Italian readers. Italian customers, a million and a half people. This is the extraction, the juice of a million and a half experiences.

What if your book does not fall into any of these categories? It is clear that if you write poetry, you can not just inspire emotions and feelings. You can hardly categorize them. But even if you write a novel, you could build a story that helps people change their lives or improve their self-esteem. And here it would fall into those categories.

If you write a medical treatise, the wellness category is the one that comes closest. Maybe without being too technical, you give it a more oriented focus on well-being, so you can reach and help more people. The key is to be flexible and adapt, without distorting.

I know that when you design a book you think that your idea is the best in the world and therefore, only for this reason, it has to sell millions of copies. But it is not so.

You have to find the right balance between your idea and the market. Because already that of readers, in Italy, is a small market; if you then choose a topic that interests little, maybe you can have your personal satisfaction, but if you do not help anyone, it makes no sense.

Here the project is more extensive, we want to help millions of people. Of course, if we help a person, that person can make a difference. But surely it is even better if we can help ten, a hundred, a thousand, a million. I also say this for you, for your return in terms of bestsellers and income.

These are the 20 categories, let your book fall into one of these. It's my editorial advice, then do as you see fit.

SECRET n. 12: structure your project so as to fit your book into one of the 20 most requested categories in Italy, finding the right balance between your idea and the market.

Bruno Editore is certainly not the only publishing house to help you in the search, even Amazon can give you a hand and inspire you, in a very simple way. Go to Amazon and look at its categories. See what the bestsellers are. You will see many books belonging to the 20 categories that I have already listed. But here you have an advantage: Amazon has dozens of sub-niches to study, on which you can specialize. And that's where you'll find inspiration.

In addition to the bestsellers, once you have identified the most suitable category for your project, download the extracts of the books for free. Perhaps you will have seen that on Amazon there is the button "Download the extract" thanks to which you can read, directly on the browser, the first pages of the book. Generally the first 10% of the book and, on 100 pages, means to be able to read a dozen.

SECRET n. 13: Amazon is an excellent source for finding new market niches and studying existing bestsellers.

Having some quick reading strategies can help, because if you want to do a research, since you are still in the process of brainstorming, you can throw down a lot of ideas; the strategy that I first adopt is to read 50 extracts of books on your topic. You can quickly get a wider view on the topic. Take a quick read of the first chapter and look at the table of contents. You need it to take inspiration, not to copy.

Read reviews, especially bestsellers, that have many, both positive and negative; there is no bestseller that has only positive reviews. When you see that there are a bit 'positive and a bit' negative, go to read the negative, to understand the points of improvement of that book and perhaps even that sector. Because that negative review could give you an idea for your book.
For example, in the books on the Law of Attraction, I noticed that all the reviews were "yes, good, but too much theory". So I wrote a book called The New Law of Attraction (Bruno Editore, 2009), which is a manual full of practical exercises and goes to fill the void left by all the other books.

It is not difficult, look. People tell you what they want. And if you have experience in that field, you can fill in the blanks and write your bestseller. If it's not your field, you should not even have gotten to read the reviews. Find an uncovered sub-niche, something on which there is still nothing. In Italy it is easier, while in the United States there are 5 million ebook, and therefore it means that there is a niche in the niche of the niche.

Some time ago I found an ultra specialist book, only 200 pages on how to cover the Amazon ebook. More niche than that. Maybe you could write a similar book in Italian. With all the market I'm creating in the book writing business, you'd already have thousands of insured customers on a book like that. You realize?

So, from this research you can start to conceive and design the title. The title is the most important part, it is what will make the difference and that will allow people to search for it on the Amazon search engine and evaluate whether to click on it or not, based on the curiosity it arouses. For this, I will now give you advanced brand positioning strategies, the same brand positioning strategies used by large companies. I did it first for my company, when it was called Autostima.net and I turned it into Bruno Editore.

The project was born by chance, to share the lessons of life I was learning. When I became an editor, we started publishing not only my books, but also those of others. We have expanded to various issues, including professional and financial growth, and Autostima.net was no longer the right name or the right brand.

So what did I do? I have downloaded 50 books on brand positioning, I have studied them all and have distorted my company. I have acted in different ways, including redoing the brand and relaunching the brand.

This expertise remained with me and I collected it in a book, *Positioning Your Brand* (Bruno Editore, 2008), the first brand positioning book ever published in Italy. Today, thanks to this book, these topics are very common among trainers and entrepreneurs.

All I am giving you and I will give you in the next pages is the result of my work, my books and my company. The exact opposite of the consultants-gurus you find out there. There are marketing experts, who have followed a course and think about getting their hands on your business, making huge disasters. As well as bank advisors, who have never invested one euro of their own pocket, they want to manage your money. A true paradox.

The marketing consultant who has studied marketing at Harvard knows the theory, but has never applied it to a company, has never spent sleepless nights because his company does not invoice.

So, all I will give you is based on what I went through first as an author of 25 bestsellers and then as a publisher of over 600 books. That's why I know you'll find interesting things here.

And now you will see the three key points for brand positioning of a book, which I have called *Book Brand Positioning*.

SECRET n. 14: the 3 secrets of *Book Brand Positioning* allow you to get an excellent and unique title.

And here are the three secrets:
1. *Be the first.*
2. *Create the niche.*
3. *Choose a unique name.*

1. *Be the first*

Who was the first man to set foot on the moon? Neil Amstrong, we all know it more or less. The second one? "Boh" is the typical answer, because people only remember the first one. No one remembers the second, also because, as we often say, "the second is only the first of the last".

The same is true for the web: you are the first in search engines or you are nobody and you lose 90% of clicks. On search engines, most of the clicks go to the first result, then a little bit to the second, then to the third and so on. In life, you are the first or you are nobody, you are a simple follower, one that follows and that pursues the first.

You do not know how many clones, immediately after the first edition of the course, have copied my Numero1 ™ program on how to write a book and become a Bestseller Author. But what's the point? If you have not been the first, just make a bad impression and destroy your brand. Become the "script" by definition.

It counts who first arrives on the market, in the mind of customers and people. Facebook was not the first social network. What social networks were there before Facebook? Myspace, one of the most widespread. You were there on Myspace? Probably not, if you're not a web pioneer.

Instead, who is on Facebook? All. You know what I mean? Facebook is the social network par excellence, the first that has arrived at all, the first that obliges you to use the real name, the first that allows you to connect friends in real time. This is the first, the first that has arrived in everyone's mind.

Likewise, Google was not the first search engine. First I told you about IOL, Arianna, Altavista, all born before; but what is the first search engine that everyone has unquestionably started using? The first true search engine, the one that really worked, was Google.

SECRET n. 15: if you want your book to be the number one, you must be the first in the minds of readers to position yourself on that topic.

Bruno Editore did not invent the ebooks, nor did I invent them; in the United States exist for years, I was nothing but a user and an ebook buyer. But I was the first to bring them to Italy, the first to introduce the e-book, to hold conferences in fairs, conventions and so on. The first to reach millions of people.

I still remember those conferences. An incredible effort because, when I brought ebooks to Italy, they slaughtered me. Imagine a young boy with a completely innovative idea that can annoy publishing giants. Those who, if the paper business goes bankrupt, are passed off; already they are bad, go to bother them, they inevitably end up hating you.

But I went ahead anyway, because I believed in my project; I started as a customer and then I knew it was the right thing, because the ebook had changed my life and could even change it to other people. So I went on my way and, in the end, I won my battle.

It's been almost ten years before the elephants of publishing understood that the digital market was exploding. Jeff Bezos was needed to say "the ebook has passed the books". When you are the number one and you are the first in everyone's head, even the colossus must give up and, if you have to choose where to start, call for advice. So it happened when a well-known paper publisher decided to start the adventure in digital. He entrusted me with his first publications in ebook.

I invite you to do the same thing in your niches. How can you be the first in the minds of your customers and readers?

Because, once you are the first, nobody can scratch you. I'll give you an example of a computer keyboard. Do you know that the keyboard you use is called qwerty? It is called this because it corresponds to the sequence of the first keys.
But nobody uses the qwerty keyboard anymore, because it was born to slow down, not to speed up. In typewriters, if you went too fast, you would break the hammer, so a key arrangement was designed to slow down. The qwerty, in fact. But it was the first keyboard and, as such, became the standard.

There are faster keyboards that are used in these races, like the Dvorak, but they are not the standard, so no one uses them and no computer manufacturer would dare change the layout of the keys. We all went crazy.

Was Windows the first window operating system? No, but it was for most of us; almost no one started with a Mac. And Steve Jobs had taken it from Xerox, so none of them invented it. Nonetheless, Windows, even in the very apt name, "windows", has arrived in computers all over the world.

The window system, for most people, Bill Gates invented it, even if it is not. But it was the first person in the minds to explode and make incredible billing. Even today, Bill Gates is the richest person in the world thanks to this intuition.

2. Create the niche

If the goal is to become number one and be the first in your niche, how can you be the first, if today there is already everything for everyone? Looking for something, do a search on Amazon, and you realize that there is already. What do you invent? Maybe it's too late because the market is saturated? If you know what makes you different from others, you can go and create your own niche, your sub-niche, and it does not matter if it's small, because you'll be the number one of that niche and you'll explode in that niche.

The ebooks did not exist and therefore the niche was non-existent; When I created the ebooks, I went directly to the sub-niche, the ebooks for training.

Even then I thought that sooner or later everyone would have done ebook and going to compete with the big publishing houses would have been difficult. But I positioned myself as the number one for training ebooks. There were not only editors of training and, even when the giants would have started making ebooks, I was already that of ebooks for training. So the brand has held even when, between 2009 and 2012, all publishers arrived on that market.

Today, specialization is everything. The other day I played at the Allegro Chirurgo with my daughter and her friends and I asked myself a very simple question: who would you be choosing for a knee surgery? The primary care physician or the knee surgeon surgeon? The specialized one, it is obvious.

Who do you want to learn how to cover a book? From someone who explains just how to write a book or from what he wrote an entire 200-page book on how to create a cover for Amazon? The more you go on to specialize, the better. The more technical you are, the better. There is a sub-niche for everyone.

And if not individuals, you create it, as did Red Bull, who created a new category. There were no "energy drinks", it was Red Bull who invented them. So the real key is to create the category.

Steve Jobs what did he do with the iPad? He created the category of tablets. Some attempts had already been made to produce the tablets, but nobody wanted them. I remember a Samsung device, rather strange and was written with the nib. But when Jobs created and launched the iPad, the world has changed.

I remember that presentation well, go look for it on YouTube, it's extraordinary. What did he do? He put the iPhone on the left, the MacBook on the right, then divided them with an empty space and made the iPad appear, creating the new category of tablets also visually. Crazy: if you wanted a tablet, it was the iPad. In just a few minutes, it has sold millions of tablets all over the world.

The differentiation can also concern the distribution model. Dell was the first computer manufacturer to sell them directly over the phone, halving costs and doubling performance, and soon became the world's first computer manufacturer. Now it is in crisis because with the Internet everyone makes direct sales, but Dell was the first to order the computer by telephone. On all the specialized magazines, I remember well, on the front page there was Dell, with incredible offers and performances.

Do you know Arnold Coffee, the chain of American coffee shops that customers have renamed the Italian Starbucks? He is present in Milan, Florence and Rome. I am one of the biggest financing partners. Think about what we have been through. You have to open a chain of cafes in

Italy, where there is a billion bars, how can you be unique? How do you specialize and build a brand in the bar industry? You study the market, you know that in the world there are several chains that work great, and bring the same concept in our country. Go in countertendency: not Italian espresso coffee, but American coffee. An incredible success.

Do you understand how the secrets of big successful companies can help you in choosing the title? In Bruno Editore, after having published the first 100 books, a difficulty arose: all the categories were taken, all the same proposals arrived. There was the book on bodybuilding, the one on how to build the perfect physical form, then came that other on how to get fit ... in short, all the same. And we rejected them all.

The message we have given is: you must specialize. Does bodybuilding already exist? Make me a book about abdominals only. The niche is small, but you will see that people will arrive, and those who want to strengthen the abs, will not buy the general bodybuilding book, but will want the specific one on the abdominals.

SECRET n. 16: for your book, create your own sub-niche, even if small, so as to be the first and only one in the industry.

3. Choose a unique name
In the third phase we analyze the name, which is incredibly important. I've already told you about the transition from Autostima.net to Bruno

Editore, and I'll give you other examples of great companies and bestselling books, so you can understand what it really means to create a high-impact name.

Pay attention to these two names: Kleenex and Scotch. Do you think these are commonly used words? For example we can say "pass me the scotch" or "give me a kleenex", but these two terms are actually the brands, that is the names of the companies that, respectively, have invented the paper handkerchief and the adhesive tape. With such power that the company name has become a word of common use. Crazy. This happens when a brand works and enters people's heads.

The beauty is that it happened to me with my book Marketing Training (Bruno Editore, 2015), which has a completely invented name. In the combination of "formative marketing", the word "formative" did not exist. If you were doing a Google search two years ago, it gave you an error and told you "maybe you were looking for information". It did not exist on the web and Google reported it as an error.

Today, it is normal to talk about educational marketing, I have held dozens of training courses and masters, and has entered strongly in people's minds. Those who work or do web marketing have heard of it, recognize it immediately, because the word comes from training, therefore, a type of marketing that forms the customer through the contents.

It has become a commonly used word, there are people who claim to apply marketing to their business, and not because they refer to my book, but because they consider it a term acquired. It is actually a registered trademark of mine, filed with the Trademarks and Patents Office. But I am more than happy that it has become a word in common use.

This is what I would like you to do when you choose the title: create a name that tomorrow will be considered normal and that represents your own sub-niche.

SECRET n. 17: Choose a powerful name for your niche and the title of your book and it will be a sure success.

The success of the title is all the more powerful, the more you stay focused on your choices and your category. So if you write a book about diet today, you should not write one about marketing tomorrow.

Why do I tell you this? Because I did it too, and it's a mistake. I want to tell you also my mistakes, so you can take advantage of my experience. I wrote 25 books on different themes, and it's not a great choice of branding, but I did it because I turned my life into a book. For example, at a certain point I decided to lose a few extra pounds, I became passionate about dieting, I read 100 books on diets and, as I obtained results, I wrote my book.

Fast Diet 3X (Bruno Editore, 2010) is one of my best-selling books and is the diary of my diet. I have achieved extraordinary results, which are useful to thousands of people, however it is not my main brand, so theoretically it is a mistake. But the willingness to share results and help people is so strong that I decided to publish it anyway. It is my mission.

As an author I made 25 books, I can write books and I can teach you to write them, but try to stay focused. The first thing that comes to mind is that, being able to write, you can even dare more and write on 100 different topics. Better not, because in this way the brand loses its effectiveness in that sector.

Rather, create a series: the first book on diet, the second on physical fitness, the third on body-building ... all topics related to the same target, so that those who bought the first book will also buy the second and the third of the series, because you know yourself as an expert in the field, you liked it and so on.

This also increases visits to Amazon, which promotes related. Have you seen the Amazon banners? Those with the words "who bought this has also bought this other", "who saw this also saw this other". If you have a necklace, this helps, because Amazon associates them automatically.

The focus was also the mantra of Steve Jobs. Do you know that he had been ousted by Apple? I do not know if you've seen the movie, read the book or if you know its history, but at one point it was thrown out of its own company. He's been out for about ten years.

When they called him back, he took all the Apple products, threw them in the bucket and decided that, from then on, they would only produce four computers. Yes, four computers, two large and two small, two for normal consumers and two for business. Nothing else. Not the dozens of models that were there before and that confused the user.

Who owns an Apple Watch? In a few, because there are too many models. And Steve Jobs would never have approved. They really did too many models - like the one worth 20,000 euros in gold - and so they made it difficult to choose. No, it's really too much, let's go back to the origins: a few things done well.

When I changed the logo and the brand in Bruno Editore, I removed everything that was not ebook. I did a lot of coaching, consulting, dozens of courses in the communication classroom: all gone. Bruno Editore was just ebook, period. I gave up a 30% turnover to relaunch the brand but, believe me, the money arrived multiplied already the following year. So, courageous choices lead to important results.

I'll tell you the story of Kellogg's. In 2012, Kellogg's bought the Pringles brand for 2.7 billion dollars. What does it mean? Kellogg's is cereal, health, healthy breakfast. Pringles, instead? It's all but health: fried potato. So associating these brands is madness. Unfortunately even the big brands can make mistakes, and they do it. Perhaps because they are too big and need to satisfy other needs such as investors, the stock exchange and a whole host of other dynamics.

Is it a differentiation? Of investment, of money, certainly yes, but if you really need to differentiate, invest in something useful. Rather, you buy yourself a development company, just to name one. If I had to buy a company, I would buy one specialized in VR (virtual reality) to create educational ebooks in virtual reality. They still do not exist, so it could be a millionaire idea. This would make sense.

Another big mistake is: Smart is the best-selling small car in Rome, in Milan and in big cities, because parking anywhere, you put it sideways. A few years ago he also produced the Smart ForFour, do you remember? They bought it in a few time, so they took it off the market. But I do not know what a bizarre choice, two years ago they decided to propose it again and they bought it from my friends. In fact, the other day, they told me that the Smart Smart was better. They were ultra pentiti.

That's it, because if you're looking for a parked car, it's the small one; if you have to do the "Big Smart", then any car is fine, it's not Smart anymore, you can buy anything from it.

So the brand is focusing. It is as if Harley Davidson were making cars; would kill the brand for which it is known and for which it has grown: the bike. Therefore, stay focused. Marketing Training is an example of focusing and being the first in its category, because I invented it, it did not exist. Yes, there is the macro category "marketing" and the sub-category "training marketing". But how many books do you know about educational marketing? Only one, mine. The name is unique because I created it.

Fast reading 3X is another of my books that sold the most. Yet fast reading really exists for many years. I did a course in 1990, when I was thirteen, so it means that it has existed for at least thirty years.

There are skilled trainers who have been doing this for decades, then I come with my book, and sell more than any other book on the market. It sells more than anything else in that sector. Why? For the marketing system behind it, as well as for the particular name, which already makes you understand that triple the speed of reading.

I was also the first to use Facebook to promote fast reading. With my advertising campaign I reached 2 million people in the first week of launch, against a very small budget. To reach 2 million people on TV, perhaps in the early evening, you need a hundred times bigger budget. And all for a result that is not even measurable, because you do not know how many people will buy your product.

Instead, with the Internet or Facebook, reach 2 million people who, with little money, click, go to the site and buy. You know exactly how many.

SECRET n. 18: The marketing you use for your book can be a differentiating factor and get you first very quickly.

So, for the title of your book, I highly recommend making this association: take the name of the general category - for example marketing, diet, self-esteem, motivation, sport - and create a new name for your specialization.

TITLE = CATEGORY + SPECIALIZATION

"Training Marketing" is the classic example: "marketing" (category) + "training" (specialization). And also "Writing" (category) "Fast 3X" (specialization). At the last master in Marketing Training, where I explained this thing, do you know what idea came out? "Food Water".

This entrepreneur is responsible for selling household sewage treatment plants, which is an extremely crowded market of competitors. But now it is the only one that owns a plant to produce "food water". I, as a customer, hearing this word would like to know more, maybe I would download his book that explains all the differences between the waters, the fixed residue and its uniqueness, of course. And I would decide to buy its 2,000 euro water purifiers. See how the whole process starts from a name and a right title?

One of my bestsellers, Making money online in 7 days (Bruno Editore, 2006), is the book from which most Italian marketers started. From there, however, I too had to specialize; to continue the series I wrote Make money online with blogs, Make money online with eBay, Make money online with Google and so on.

So, specialize. For example, I do not think there are books on how to make money with WhatsApp. Or with Telegram. It would be a bestseller. If I am an entrepreneur and show me that these tools are explosive for my business, I would buy your book. And I would also buy videocourses and consultations to learn more or to get help to apply the new marketing system to my business.

You know what I mean? I'm already giving you ideas that alone are worth a thousand times the cover price of this book, it's up to you now to put them into practice.

In the following pages, I will suggest you some titles and surely you will not be the only one who wants to develop them. In fact, it would not surprise me if Amazon was soon filled with titles on how to do business with WhatsApp or Telegram.

Open Amazon and take the bestsellers in the "diet" category. Here are the titles: 3x fast diet, longevity diet, fat-free recipes and so on. You want to write a recipe book but there are millions of them. What can you do with one? The first recipe book without fat, as in this example. Or again, to lose weight by walking, intermittent fasting. What does it mean? What should I do every other day? This title is trying to intrigue me, to intrigue me. Maybe I'm looking for a book on fasting, this title hits me and, if I think it's my case, I'll buy it with a click.

Then I could discover that the author is very good, that I like how he explains and that there is also a link to go to his site, to buy his advice, a video course or ask his opinion. If there is no link, the author is losing a big chance.

So, on one side there is the professional with no customers, who has to fight with people who do not pay, or who claims not to have customers and not know where to find them.

On the other hand, the professional arrives with the book with an appealing title and attracts an avalanche of customers. Because maybe he attended the last edition of Numero1 ™ and is simply putting my advice into practice.

In summary, the title has these purposes:
- challenge and intrigue
- contact your target

- uniqueness and differentiation
- concreteness with numbers
- optimized for Amazon search

The purpose of the title is to challenge and intrigue people. Would you not want those people to click on that card of the book and be intrigued to the point of buying it?

Think of a title like that of Alfio Bardolla's bestseller: Money makes happiness. It is very provocative, since people have always thought that money does not make happiness and instead he tells you yes. So, or you're not particularly sympathetic, or buy it, which happens often, since it has sold 300,000 copies of his books.

Also you have to address your target, so already from the title people have to understand what you sell and what you're talking about. There are absurd titles on Amazon, and in fact you find them at the hundredth or thousandth position of the category. They're right down because they do not sell a copy.

The title must be unique and different, and you can add the numbers, because they always give concreteness. For example, 39 public speaking techniques would attract more than if there were no specific number. Or 500 recipes without fat. The numbers work.

Finally it is very important to optimize the search on Amazon; to be the first, you must enter the keywords in the title. So, as much as you can be creative as advertisers do, you need to be practical and put those keywords in your headline.

Therefore, a title like the one in my series Making Money Online is a little trivial, it's not fascinating, but it contains several keywords that people are looking for. Whether it's "money", "making money", "making money online", "money online", any combination works. This is why it is one of my most downloaded bestsellers.

SECRET n. 19: a working title must be curious, must address the right target, must be unique, must contain numbers and more keywords.

Where are the keywords? What are they? I do not speak only of those you have in mind, which are related to your topic, but of those that people really seek. Those that your 600 million credit card Amazon customers are looking for right now.

The great news is that Amazon gives you free access to the research database. Yes, for free. As long as you go on the search engine, put the word that could be in your category, for example "diet", and that returns you, in real time and in order of sales and the most searched words, the combinations that contain the term "diet".

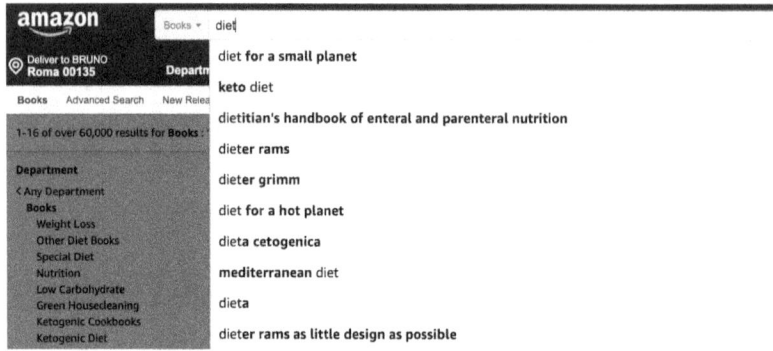

If you are looking for "diet", Amazon suggests: longevity diet, mima fasting diet, weight loss diet, ketogenic diet, fasting diet, blood type diet, zone diet.

So, if you're an area diet expert, what do you do? Write the keywords that Amazon considers most suitable for your sector, put them all together and create a title that contains all or almost all.

This regards Amazon. And Google? It does the exact same thing: it suggests the most searched keywords on Google. It has a billion users and therefore, although they are not all buyers, the results are more than reliable.

Go gle   diet

diet **sapienza**
diet **traduzione**
diet **plan**
diet **definition**
healthy diet
open diet
diet **moduli**
email diet

Focusing on the word diet: find weekly diet, meaning diet, diet Wikipedia. These last two interest us little to sell a book, instead "fast weight loss diet" is a good keyword.

So, how do you behave? You write them. What are the most interesting you've seen? Diet, longevity, fasting, slimming, area, weekly, balanced, lose weight quickly and so on.

You must create a title and a subtitle that contains these keywords. Not all, maybe one, two or three. If you're all good too. Do you want a title that contains all of them?

It took me a while to put them all together, but I did it: Balanced weight loss diet. 52 weekly recipes in the area, to increase longevity and lose weight fast and without fasting. Best seller!

Incredible, in any search on Amazon such a title would always appear, even for different combinations of keywords. So, when you decide the title and the subtitle, think carefully and enter the right keywords, the most sought after ones.

Amazon advises you what the customers, who pay by credit card and want to buy that book, are looking for. If they find yours, what will they ever do? If the presentation or cover is not bad, they will buy it. Point.

This information also applies if you write a novel. People do not look for the title, because the titles of the novels are totally invented. So, unless you're already famous, people will not be looking for your title or you as an author.

What are people looking for? Either go by category, or insert in the search engine "novel", then choose the related sub-categories: "yellow novel", "romance novel", "erotic novel" and so on.

These are the key words that people, in order of importance, look for on Amazon in this sector: historical novel, criminal, ghost, erotic, gay, rose, romance. For the same narrative: contemporary history, Italian, for children, erotica. We do not publish it, but my old idea was to found a publishing house of erotic stories. In my opinion it would sell a lot, and the searches on Amazon confirm it to me.

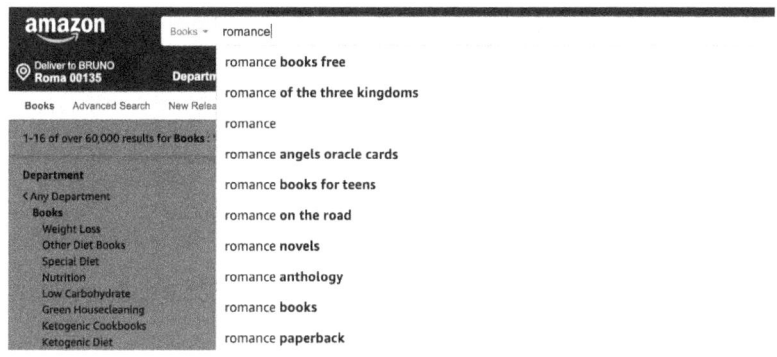

So, we collect the key words: novel, historical, criminal, ghost, eroticism, rose, Italian, yellow. Here, putting them all together is impossible, because either you make a romance novel, or a romance novel, or an erotic novel. You can not do everything together. Oh yeah?

I tried with my students at the last edition of the Numero1 ™ course and we were able to do it. Here is the title that contains all the keywords: La Rosa Del Criminale. The first yellow novel in the Italian historical context, including ghosts, eroticism and secret services. It's the perfect title for a novel.

The beauty is that, during the event, a person has offered to write it really and in less than a month he has completed it. And when we launched it, it immediately became a bestseller. As expected, it was really a great success.

SECRET n. 20: the inclusion in the title of the most sought after keywords on Amazon is essential to be found and become bestsellers, both for training books and for novels and fiction.

So your goals are the title and the subtitle. What interests me is what you, as a customer, would look for in your sector. If you take care of weddings, what would you look for? "How to have a lasting relationship", "marriage", "marriage tips". Put all these keywords together and take out your title.

To create your bestseller, it is extremely important to make an accurate selection of the title and keywords. Thanks to a suitably chosen title, from here to 3/6 months your book may have already become an Amazon bestseller. Imagine the cover of your book with the title you wrote, with your name on it and the "Author Bestseller" logo. Extraordinary.

I believe in it, I believe in you and in your project, and I'm sure that in a short time you can achieve this result. If you commit yourself, you can do it in just 30 days. I will show you the techniques to design the book and write it quickly.

Speed is important, because things are quick or you are likely to postpone them forever. When you are strongly motivated, you do not want to postpone. For me speed is really a mantra, because it represents my orientation to the result. If I have to study a subject, I quickly read 50 books, because I want to learn everything immediately. In the same way, when I write, I write quickly because I can not wait to publish my book.

Every time I have a new idea, I'm there writing, writing, writing and still writing. Maybe for a year I do nothing and then in two weeks I write a new book from scratch.

I do not know how long life will last and I want to hurry up. I do not know if I will have time to complete all my projects and for this I would like to finish them tomorrow. I do my own the philosophy of "living as if it were the last day".

Do it yourself, with this intensity, and see how your dedication will bear fruit. So now concentrate and throw down ideas for your title.

TITLE:

_____

_____

SUBTITLE:

_____

_____

_____

AMAZON & GOOGLE KEY WORDS:

_____
_____
_____
_____
_____
_____
_____
_____
_____

Done? I know how the choice of the title is not a simple thing. Indeed it is the most delicate and important of all, to have a successful book.

This is why I want to bring you a series of examples taken from authors who have attended my courses in the Numero1 ™ classroom, so that you can learn from the mistakes of others.

Once a participant told me that he was writing a book reserved for aesthetic professionals. The title chosen was: Zone aesthetics is dead. Surely he intrigued me. I do not know what the area looks like, but to say that "something is dead" works. In one of my famous article on the marketing marketing blog I wrote "the word of mouth is dead" and I had an amazing success, with thousands of shares. It's a strong statement, and a book that has such a title can be interesting.

Following this he also offered me a second version of that title: Aesthetics a thousand. Let's say that I found it a bit weak as a title. Aesthetics is the general category, but the method is missing. Formative aesthetics would be better. Maybe I do not know her and, if I were part of the world of aesthetics, I would like to know more. It could be an innovative method in which, while they give you a treatment, they teach you things, so that you can do it by yourself. And here is where a new brand is born and a chain can be created. Aesthetics a thousand, personally, I do not communicate anything new. So you have to work on finding something in which you are unique, in your work, in your business, something that only you can do, and put it in the title.

I also report another case, that of a lady who wrote a book entitled The Woman and the Nine Months of Sweet Expectation: How to Live Pregnancy with Happiness and Gratitude through the Three T Method. She also wanted to explain what the book was about, but my answer was negative. I explained to her that I am nothing but a simple Amazon user, and there is no contact between me and the author of a book. When a person navigates on Amazon, it is not that he can ask for explanations. See the title and the cover. If he is not attracted to it, it goes further.

Returning to the analysis of the title, I found it a bit 'too generic, with many keywords but unattractive, similar to many others. Surely, however, I can say that I was intrigued by the "method of the three T", so my advice was to bring it in the title, not in the subtitle. I suggested you turn it into Pregnancy 3T. How to live the nine months of sweet waiting with happiness and gratitude. Basically I exchanged title and subtitle and followed the scheme of uniting category and specialization.

The cases that you report are never enough, because they are very educational and can help you to correct any mistakes, so I'll give you more. The title of another boy's book was The journey to happiness, with subtitle Find self-esteem and courage starting from scratch. Now, I want to point out to you, as I pointed out to him, how this title is too general.
In the research phase it is important to look for titles similar to ours; if you are looking for "happiness" or "self-esteem", you will find many titles similar to this, and it will be difficult to distinguish it from others. It is a very common mistake.

The reader finds 50 similar titles and, at that point, maybe goes for reviews, scores, stars. However, if you started from scratch with your book, you do not have any reviews, stars, or visibility, so you'll never be able to stand on top and stand out. We need to be more concrete, work more on the concept of brands; what you have to do is invent something that does not exist. As in training marketing, you can create a title of the type Felistima from scratch, creating a real brand with a new word. The starting point is this.

Then I happened to talk with a guy who deals with network marketing and wrote a title on the topic Network Marketing PRO with Facebook and social media, with subtitle How to earn three thousand two hundred euros annuity, with a job online from home and finally discover the true profession of your life.

I told him that no doubt there are not many books of this type, and that therefore has little competition and could be interesting. After all I know the sector and I can confirm that on the strategies for doing Network Marketing through Facebook there is very little, so it will tend to emerge regardless.

However, I pointed out that this too was a bit generic. In the first instance the problem did not exist, but it could have occurred later, if another ten people had done the same thing and had dealt with online Network Marketing. The suggestion I gave him was to focus on that keyword: PRO. Facebook PRO could make the difference as a method in the title.

Let's move on to another case, an accountant who wrote a book, left in the drawer for four years, entitled A concept of formative experiences and life to share with your child, with subtitle How to communicate with your child. The problem here was in the choice of the title and the subtitle, because according to him the long one was the title and the shorter one the subtitle, while in reality it had to be quite the opposite.

Reasoning; the concept is nothing more than "communicating with your child", therefore, what is the category? The relationship between parents and children. But here too the problem of the brand remains. In fact it is not enough to write "communicate with your child", because it is too general. We need to invent something even more innovative. The example I gave to that accountant was that of one of our bestsellers called Parent Coach. A very apt brand that, once again, combines the general category (parents) with specialization (coach).

Another case that happened to me was that of an entrepreneur in the training sector who, in particular, was involved in European projects. The title of his book was Working with Erasmus. How to create a paying and profitable profession with European funds.

At first glance it seems an interesting title, but for the sake of it I have also asked him if maybe he was informed about someone else who had written something like that, then about possible competitors. His response was perspicacious, stating that yes, books existed on European funds, but they were also very technical, far from his idea of creating something that was focused, instead, on Erasmus.

Surely someone like him has an advantage, because in Italy there is not as much competition as in the United States, and starting from quite small niches, like that of Erasmus, makes it easy to find a title and be successful.

Another case is that of a boy who had attended high school, who until then had been an engineer, just like me, and wanted to change jobs. The title of his book immediately caught my attention; short and concise: The future has passed. I could not say what it was, but as a first impression I liked it and caught my attention. If I, who am a curious person, were browsing on Amazon, I would click on that title to learn more.

The last case is that of a gentleman who proposed me two versions and two different titles. The first was Solve your problems by telling them and the alternative was "Problem Telling". This second title remained in my mind, because it was particular and reflected precisely the concept that I have explained so far, in these pages, namely to create a new word, a different approach.

We talk a lot about storytelling, telling stories to sell and persuade and Problem Telling I really enjoyed it, it's a new word, original and already explains in the title of what it is about. It was a great title and did not require any changes on my part. He could also use the other title Solve your problems by telling them as a subtitle of the book.

The title is therefore really the most important tool you have to get noticed, get out of anonymity and turn a simple idea into a global success. So check out what you wrote in the first exercise or, if you have not already done so, take 10/15 minutes to do it carefully. It is definitely the most important part of your whole project.

SUMMARY OF CHAPTER 2:

- SECRET n. 11: Do a thorough inner research to understand what you are experienced, what you like to do and what results you have achieved in life.
- SECRET n. 12: structure your project so as to fit your book into one of the 20 most requested categories in Italy, finding the right balance between your idea and the market.
- SECRET n. 13: Amazon is an excellent source for finding new market niches and studying existing bestsellers.
- SECRET n. 14: the 3 secrets of *Book Brand Positioning* allow you to get an excellent and unique title.
- SECRET n. 15: if you want your book to be the number one, you must be the first in the minds of readers to position yourself on that topic.
- SECRET n. 16: for your book, create your own sub-niche, even if small, so as to be the first and only one in the industry.
- SECRET n. 17: Choose a powerful name for your niche and the title of your book and it will be a sure success.
- SECRET n. 18: The marketing you use for your book can be a differentiating factor and get you first very quickly.
- SECRET n. 19: a working title must be curious, must address the right target, must be unique, must contain numbers and more keywords.
- SECRET n. 20: the inclusion in the title of the most sought after keywords on Amazon is essential to be found and become bestsellers, both for training books and for novels and fiction.

Chapter 3
How to map the writing project

So far we have seen the extreme importance of the choice of the title. It is at the base of everything, it represents the first cells of the child that is being born. But if the title is the first phase, we must now structure the summary and the contents.

Writing a book does not mean sitting in front of a computer and writing, because you would not know where to start. There, the writer's block arrives. I tried it myself at the beginning, fifteen years ago: I put myself there, but nothing. The title is not enough for you to write, it gives you a first idea but, if you want to get to your destination, you need a clear and defined map.

The title is fine, it is as if I had taken the boat and I had gone out in the middle of the sea. But where do you want to get there? What is the path? What is the most correct way? Because if you do not have this map, do not arrive at your destination. You can take the longest and most luxurious yacht of all, but if you do not have a direction, it will not get you anywhere.
Don't you believe it? Before explaining any design strategy, I want you to try to write a page of your book, taking into account all the feelings

that inspire you. In a few minutes, without having yet designed anything, without knowing what you will write, only based on the title you have created so far.

I tell you in advance that it may happen that you come across the writer's block and can not write anything but a few lines. I did this exercise with some participant of Numero1 ™ and the feelings were different: those who felt joy and desire to continue to write, who confusion, those who fear to write trivia, who anxiety and fear of emptiness, who wants to finish, who emotion, who has the impression of not being up to it and who, finally, has felt a sense of freedom.

What I want is to bring out the emotions, those visceral sensations that you may have inside, that do not come out or that you are not used to telling or sharing.

Write the first page of your book:

_____

_____

_____

_____

_____

_____

_____

_____

Often to eliminate any negative feelings, it would be enough to imagine writing a letter to a friend. It's fantastic, because, as I told you in the previous pages, every day we write hundreds of words in our emails and it's easy. Zero anxieties.

Start by creating your book by imagining writing a letter to a friend or wanting to help a person. Imagine an ideal person who is there, ready to be helped by your knowledge and your book. You will realize that you can easily overcome any type of block. This thing then we will deepen also in the chapter dedicated to fast writing techniques.

In any case, when writing, feelings can be many, but overcome them as you write. Write a page, then write the second, third, maybe even at the end of the book; You could still feel tension because you do not know how it will go.

You do not know it, but you did your best, you put your emotions, your stories, your experiences, your sharing and someone will appreciate it; and maybe he will write to you, giving you positive feedback for having changed his life.

It is no longer just about becoming a bestseller on Amazon, but of having changed a person's life, which is ultimately the most important thing. Try to live already with this idea in mind: thanks to the strategies that I will give you, your book will be a masterpiece and will become a bestseller. So it is already a certainty that your work today, a tomorrow will have helped many people.

SECRET n. 21: start writing a book can give life to a thousand sensations, negative or positive, that will give you the push to complete your work and publish your book.

The solution is very simple: in this book I am going to give you clear strategies, a specific project, a guide that will accompany you step by step. They are all strategies tested in fifteen years of experience.

I also used them with my daughter, who had a homework during the last Christmas holidays: writing her holiday diary. No specific task was simply the classic "take a notebook and every day write a little page of what you did during the holidays".

Of course, just as we adults wait until the last moment, she did the same thing. So the first week she did almost nothing, partly because we were on vacation, we were out, had fun and her mind was far from homework. As soon as we got home and decided to start doing homework, she took the notebook and burst into tears.

Why? Because he did not know where to start. Rightly, we have the block, imagine a 7 year old girl who is learning to write well, structuring the best phrases, paying attention to the adjectives, in short, everything from scratch.

But he did not know what to write, he did not remember what he had done specifically that week, day by day, and did not know how to structure that page.

So, to reassure her, I approached her and reminded her that I wrote many books and that I teach writing. I put myself close to her with the desire to teach her to write a text, because, although it might seem boring, it is certainly a very important skill.

I told her that when I wrote the first books, I did not know where to start; until one day, at age 13, I did not discover the so-called Mind Maps. I told her I'm a wonderful, creative tool that, indeed, is made especially for children and that she would have fun, because she would have to color

and draw. So I drew a circle, in the middle I wrote "diary" and made the first branches with various colors, then she would have to fill it.

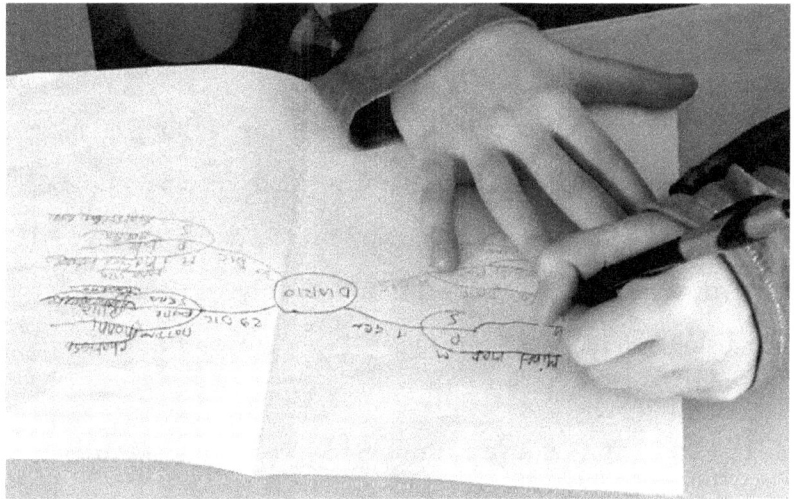

Together we have seen the days; I split the paper in the morning, afternoon and evening and helped her to rebuild what we had done the week before.

Then I told her to make a personal diary and write her map of the day every night, what she had done in the morning, what she had for lunch, what she had done in the afternoon and finally in the evening.

Every evening he wrote the key words on his map so as not to forget them and the next morning he wrote the page, perfectly reconstructing the facts. The first day I taught her this method, she wrote eight pages, recovering the whole week before! If a child has succeeded, you can do it too.

Mental Maps are an exceptional tool for planning, writing, taking notes, suitable for children too. His homework had become fun. Because learning must be fun. If you acquire notions in a boring way, you do not learn. Maps, on the other hand, are simply a different way of schematising and making a project.

SECRET n. 22: to achieve considerable results and become a true Bestseller Author, it is appropriate to structure the content well through the Mind Maps.

When I write a book, first I always do the map: the title at the center, the various chapters and then, for each chapter, I go to insert the topics. Here is an example of a map taken by MindMeister:

A completely different structure from the classic linear notes, written line by line. But it is one of the many errors that the Italian school has taught us, in writing as well as in reading. The brain is not linear, has an idea, then moves on to another; that keyword reminds him of another experience that makes him experience another experience, passing from one neuron to another, from one idea to another, all of a sudden. It is called radiant thought.

Therefore learning must reflect the functioning of the brain; it works better and is more fun. Is not this scheme any better than we are used to process or see in books? Colors stimulate creativity. You know, in fact, that we have two hemispheres: the right one of rationality and the left one of creativity. With the maps we involve both.

So it's a completely different way of reasoning, in connection with our brains. Also the topics of my courses follow the method of Mind Maps and I schematize all the courses in ultra-detailed maps.

Once I master the topic I want to deal with, I create a simplified map, with only the main branches, which is very easy to memorize and display.

To this end, I want to mention the Pareto Principle, also known as the "80-20 law", which says that 80% of the results are given by 20% of the shares. And, vice versa, 80% of the shares give 20% of the results. In any field.

In this specific case, 20% of the words give 80% of the meaning and 80% of the words are basically useless. It means that, if I only write the key words of a topic, within my map, they will be sufficient to reconstruct an entire paragraph. Ten words are enough to build an entire chapter.

This also works with fast reading. One of the things I teach is that you do not need to read everything, because most words are useless.

For example, all the articles, the conjunctions and the prepositions, the brain bypasses them, that is, it looks only at key words, nouns and creates images. This helps you learn faster and read faster; everything is based on this principle.

Even to schematize you only need a few key words to get the whole meaning. So, to realize your book you first need to schematize it with a map. Think also about the moment when you may find yourself presenting your book in a bookstore, or a group of friends. You do not have time to tell all the contents page by page, you want to display only those 3 or 4 essential concepts.

So prepare your map and it is much easier to memorize what is not the whole book. For example, I discussed my degree in engineering with the only help of my mind map. I had no books, no notes, no slides, nothing. My classmates were baseless, because in 2003 these tools were not used. Even today, many do not know them.

It was very easy to connect all the arguments, because they were all gathered in a map, in a single image that my brain had seen and reviewed dozens of times.

SECRET n. 23: 80% of the meaning of a book is given by 20% of words, so only a few key words are needed to design your book effectively.

How are the maps created? By hand, quietly, otherwise there are software of all kinds, such as MindManager, MindNode, FreeMind, MindMeister. Some are free, others have demo versions to try. The basic functions and schemes are the same for everyone, so do a few tests to see which one best meets your needs.

I suggest you use the maps for everything: work projects, objectives and, above all, your book. My life is made up of maps of everything.

Let's take the case of your 100-page book: you can draw 5 colored branches, based on a structure of 5 chapters of 20 pages each. Not too short, but not too long. For each branch you can create three sub-branches, with three topics to be discussed in that chapter. So from that chapter your reader can learn 3 essential points.

The brain struggles to handle too much information, so 3 is the perfect number of concepts relevant to each chapter. When you outline three key concepts for each chapter, you have developed 15 important topics at the end of the book.

For each branch and sub-branch, then write the most appropriate keywords to represent the concepts you want to communicate. For example, when I talk about marketing, the three important things are Facebook, Optin Page and Sales Page; if you have a book on diet, you can talk about physical activity, nutrition and integration.

You can also draw, because the image remains more impressed in the brain. If you are looking for mind maps online, you will find artistic masterpieces. Where to find inspiration to fill the map? Where to take all these topics or how to develop them?

I'll give you an example of how I structured the Numero1 ™ course, dividing it into 5 main parts: designing, writing, publishing, launching and monetizing the book. So 5 branches, 5 main topics. For each one I then added 3 contents. On how to write a book I have several topics to cover and I have included them in the sub-branches. And it is from this project that this book was born. What I teach you is how much I have put into practice for my own course.

Once you've entered your keywords, you can start searching online to see if there are other keywords already used by other authors. Check on Amazon if there are similar books. If you read so many books like me, then the research becomes immense; you have topics to speak for twenty days or to write a thousand-page book.

Obviously you have to put yours, it's not like you have to summarize twenty books. You must put your experience in that subject. From Amazon, you can download the extract of the books and read the first chapter. If you find an interesting one, done well, buy it and read it all.

And if there are no books on your topic to inspire you? If there are no bestsellers in your category, there are two possibilities:

a. You are very lucky because it is a virgin market.
b. It is an extremely negative market and is not valid as it can not be monetised. Maybe it's a subject for which people are not willing to pay. It's a little sought after market, so nobody has ever written anything, so make this assessment to see if this is the case.

But if it falls into those 20 categories that I listed before, it is certainly a book with excellent potential for profit.

On the other hand, if it is full of bestsellers it means that it is full of famous books that have sold so much and so you have a lot of competition.

SECRET n. 24: You have to find the right inspiration to fill your map and create topics through your experience.

So let's start by composing the skeleton of the book, which is fundamental: create your map with the title in the middle. I suggest you do it with the colors; buy some beautiful colored pencils as when you were a child or borrow from your children. A colored map will surely change the way you see and design your book.

And if you have more than 5 chapters? Simple, make more branches. But without exaggerating. In our experience, of many published books, of reviews, of feedback we have received, the ideal book is 5/7 chapters and the perfect chapter is 20/30 pages.

Then if they are 40 nothing changes and it is not that everyone should be exactly the same, but let's say that 20/30 is the perfect number for the length of a chapter in a 100-page book. If the book is 200 pages, like this, you can also make 40/60 page chapters. As a reference, take that of a book written in legible characters, font size 16, for the most technical, and the interline 1.5. One hundred pages of ours are 15,000 words, or 100,000 characters.

Take them as general guidelines, both on the length and the chapter titles. We, in the world of education, use a lot of chapters in style "how to ...". This is the idea, because we are planning a training book, but if you write a novel, you will obviously have another story to tell.

It's your book, write it as you please, these are just indications that work, the intent is that it is a practical book that can help people to change their lives. Because, as I will show you in these pages, when people download the extract of your book, and they will do it if they want to buy it, from the table of contents they will already understand if it is of interest to them or not.

From the summary they already understand the benefits they will find in your book, because you reveal them "how to get more in your relationship", "how to make the marriage last 150 years" and so on, and maybe that's exactly what they're looking for. The summary in which they read the list of chapters "how to" is exactly what will allow or make the person want to download and read the complete book.

Now, before continuing with the next chapter, take a few minutes to write and enrich your map, which is particularly important because it represents the project, the skeleton of your book. So, take a piece of paper, color pencils and proceed with your work.

SUMMARY OF CHAPTER 3:

- SECRET n. 21: start writing a book can give life to a thousand sensations, negative or positive, that will give you the push to complete your work and publish your book.
- SECRET n. 22: to achieve considerable results and become a true Bestseller Author, it is appropriate to structure the content well through the Mind Maps.
- SECRET n. 23: 80% of the meaning of a book is given by 20% of words, so only a few key words are needed to design your book effectively.
- SECRET n. 24: You have to find the right inspiration to fill your map and create topics through your experience.

Chapter 4
Copywriting techniques to write the text

So far we have dealt with the part of the design, while in this chapter I will enter the heart of the topic: how to write a book, your book. For many it is one of the most distressing and difficult steps, because of the anxiety, not knowing what to write or the fear of being trivial. These are normal sensations that you can consider already outdated, as I will give you the exact patterns to follow.

Let's start from the basics of writing. Many people ask me where and how to write it, whether on paper, Office Word, Mac Pages, Adobe InDesign or some pagination program. The answer is easy: the text is written simply on Word, of the Office package, basic writing program that more or less have all, or even in the free version, OpenOffice; in short, on a text editor. No complicated software.

Once, at a job interview, a girl who proposed herself as an editor asked me as perplexed as a publishing house could still use Word. That Word was obsolete to write and that you had to use advanced programs like Adobe InDesign.

I told her that everyone knows Word and we want to simplify our authors' lives, not complicate it. We can not teach the author to use complicated programs. I was the first author of my publishing house and I did not want to learn strange or particularly complex programs. I have always used Word, it has always been great and today all our authors use it, also because it is a format that easily transforms into the various other formats compatible with ebook reader and Amazon.

You can write using Word, or similar programs, from where the Doc file, the classic Word file, will come out. Then you can simply save it in PDF and your ebook is ready. Bruno Editore's ebooks have been in Pdf format for over 10 years. For some years we have been working with the Epub and Mobi formats, which are more technical and useful for ebook readers and tablets. Amazon, however, today also accepts the Doc, so you do not need anything else. If you upload the Office file, it transforms it into its format and you have no problem. Once again, Word is confirmed as number one in terms of compatibility between the various platforms.

When there is a standard, we use that, we do not have to invent anything. They are simple rules, we do not complicate things.

SECRET n. 25: in the structure of your book you can refer to various editing or layout programs, but the best remains Word for simplicity and compatibility.

The book should be structured in such a way that you can change people's lives, this is your focus. You have to generate word of mouth, so much pleasure that someone can even think of wanting to "pirate" your book, that is, to run free for groups of friends. No, I'm not kidding, it means your book is great.

In this regard, one of the great diatribes that was at the beginning in the publishing house was whether or not to protect Pdf files. And we had the unfortunate idea of protecting them with a password. So, the customer who was buying was sent the Pdf file and, attached by email, the password, so that if the file then went around, it could not be opened.

But the truth is that, to limit the damage of 1% of pirates that run online, we were instead creating a bad experience of usability and enjoyment of the product for 99% of honest people.
The thing lasted a few months because, already after the third email I received from people who honestly bought my book, but could not open it, I was fed up. They could not find the password anymore and it was not really possible to insert it on the ebook reader. So they were unusable. At this point, I thought directly to eliminate it. Files open for everyone. And trust everyone.

If then there are people who are not correct, their business, because my intent and my priority were, and still are, to offer a positive experience to people who had trusted me, who had paid to read a book of their interest . Do you agree with me? My philosophy is this: to help those who gave me confidence. Give confidence to those who are buying and reading.

In the traditional publishing world, unfortunately, this is not shared. Most traditional publishers protect their files, and the result is that the customer stops buying from them because he can not use them.

Generally I always go against the current. If mass does one thing, I do the opposite. In general I'm never wrong to follow this philosophy. In fact I am also a supporter of the money back guarantee. Almost none, only a few, do not do it in training. Many "gurus" think that if you do not like training, it is your problem and they have worked on it anyway.

Instead, I am of the opinion that it is necessary to reassure customers that if they do not like something they will get their money back. For me this means guaranteeing the people who bought and trusted me. Then it's up to me to repay them, offering them the best course possible.

Another important feature that you need to keep in mind when structuring content is the ability to sell and promote yourself, just because your book is your business card. In fact you do not do it for money, also because the royalties are never a source of significant income, but you want your book to be the most downloaded of Amazon, to build authority and visibility, and then you can also give it for free.

I learned it many years ago when I was still a beginner. Out of pure curiosity, I took one of my books by pirating it myself and put it on eMule, which was a peer-to-peer software, like Napster, where pirates and cunning traded files illegally. At the end of that book, I had put a link that reported the catalog of Bruno Editore, in affiliation. So that link traced the purchases made by those people who, appreciating my book downloaded free, clicked to learn more. Within the first 6 months my "self-pirated" book generated sales of other books for 100,000 euros. Crazy. Those same people who liked the book, clicking on that link, went to the catalog and maybe bought another 5/10 books.

Today the training marketing method I teach is the same, starting from giving a book or a Pdf. Only that it was involuntary and casual, an experiment, but today it is schematized.

You can create important automatic income through the book. No, not with the royalties that, as I told you, hardly exceed 100/200 euros per month. Especially if you give it for free as a strategy to get to thousands of people. The real profit can come if you use the book to let you know and, perhaps, propose other forms of business.

Which does not mean you have to write a fake book just to promote or sell something else. Many consultants put little content in their book, so they can sell additional paid content. No, this is not the purpose, and it does not even work.

Your book is appreciated if it's true, if it's full of content and if it changes your life to others. It must be the top of the top. Then, if there is also something else for people who want to deepen, so much the better. The customer is happy to give more money to a person who has helped him.

Take this same book: if it did not really contain the techniques that allow you to write your book quickly, would you give me further confidence? Certainly not. On the contrary, given that the book offers you concrete help, maybe you will be the first to want to study in depth in the classroom with the Numero1 ™ course. Do you therefore understand the importance of always being congruent and of having the satisfaction of readers' expectations as a priority?

One of the greatest masters, in this way of writing, is certainly Anthony Robbins. Its system starts with free high quality material; goes around, lectures, online videos, teleseminari, webinars and so on, all for free.

When you know Anthony Robbins you immediately realize that he is the number one. If one can afford it, it will go one step further and will attend one of its courses without thinking twice. I participated in what he held in London in 2005, and he overwhelmed me. He arrived in the classroom and I felt crazy energy. I came out of that classroom and changed my life again, again thanks to him.

During that course, it takes an hour to present his Mastery University. He did such a job during the previous two days, which is a pleasure to hear him talk about his flagship event. Although it is theoretically making a sale, it is still a pleasure. It is one of the most spectacular routes in the world of personal growth. It costs a lot, but it's worth a lot and I've never heard anyone complain about the shopping. It costs more not to have gone there.

This is just one of the steps. For those who can, for those who want to go further, there is the Platinum Program; it costs $ 65,000, but you are personally followed by him, you can go for private courses with him, in various islands around the world. What incredible value do you have?

However, it all started with some free content on the web or from his € 11.90 book. It's that book that changes your life. After you've read and twisted your life, then you decide you want to go all the way and be followed by the number one. No doubt we are talking about marketing, but we are also talking about radical changes in your life, and that person is able to do this on you, everything depends on the value you give him. When I find a good guy who sells me a path that will change my life, I thank him.

On the other hand, if Anthony Robbins were you, you'd be very rich. And if you're an entrepreneur or a professional, it's crazy not having written your book yet. It is the main tool of our century to let you know and appreciate yourself and your business.

So it is important to build a similar system even in the small of your niche, without being Anthony Robbins; because maybe 5/10 thousand euro a month more can generate them and can change your life enormously.

SECRET n. 26: evaluate to give your book also free to generate word of mouth, build authoritativeness and create very important automatic income.

This only happens if you hit people deep down, so always give the maximum content, without omitting other things out of fear that the next product will not be bought. If I then want to deepen my client or I need to talk with you, I'll get advice. I am ready to follow you all the way, provided that at the base there is always a great ethical value.

This means that you have to structure the book to keep the promise that your title makes to the reader. So, if you teach how to lose weight fast, you have to provide the right strategies. If you write a book on diet, before even thinking about what to sell later, the reader you have to really lose weight. Then if he liked the mode, he will ask you for extra products or advice.

Follow this lineup that is the same that I use for my books. Are you ready? Here is the structure and *copywriting* for high impact books:

- Challenge and tell him something he does not know.
- Talk about the opportunity / goal.
- Explain the problem and shake it.
- Anticipate the objections / dispel the myths.
- From value strategies to achieve the goal.
- Tell your story or about other people you've helped.
- Explain the path to deepen.

Start with a challenge, because on the one hand you have already captured the attention of the person with the title, on the other you start with an effect concept. In my Fast *Reading 3X* book I start with: "Do you know that you can read one page per second?" I'm challenging your mind, I'm telling you that you can have and do more.

Continuing with the example of fast reading, then I talk about the opportunity: "Did you know that we do not use the brain for what it really is? Some research says that we use only 10% of the brain and it is certainly true that we use it little.

There are strategies that can help us increase our ability to read, understand and memorize ».

SECRET n. 27: immediately involve your reader by challenging him and telling him about the opportunity he will have in reading your book.

And again: «So, why is it important to read quickly? Because you can read a lot of books that could change your life. If you are already reading just one book a week, in a year you have read 52 books and you are one of the leading experts in your field. If you are a seller today and read 52 books on the sale, in a year you are another person. If you have problems with self-esteem today, read 52 books on personal growth and in a year you are another person. " This can be the introduction of a book on fast reading.

Then we move on to the question of the problem: what is the problem that you and your readers have to face? "As you know, today's world goes very fast and, if you're still, so if you do not evolve and do not read new books, stay where you are." This is a nice problem.

Then we anticipate the objections: "Many think that reading quickly makes you lose your understanding and then you do not understand anything. I also thought so, then, with some immediate techniques that I will teach you in five minutes, in the third chapter you will have already learned to read 3 times faster ».

It's a good promise, but I know I can keep it, so I write it. Among other things, if my reader has downloaded the free excerpt, he is reading only my introduction and already knows that in the third chapter I will give him a technique that, in five minutes, in an immediate way, will triple the reading speed. And that book is already sold, because it keeps an important promise.

Then give him the strategies. So, of 100 pages, the first ten are introduction, opportunity and various, followed by 80/90 pages of content. You do not have to do just self-promotion, but focus on providing content and strategies to help others. The content must make it independent and keep the promise you made in the introduction and the title, as well as in the book.

SECRET n. 28: always provide maximum content and value strategies, so that the reader is completely independent of that topic.

Then share with your stories and your results in the field. Because what really interests readers is what you did. Even the best trainer in the world will ask you if he has also adopted this technique, if he just teaches or if he has really succeeded.

So consistency is very important, and insert it into the book, through the stories of what you've been through, you've lived, you've done, you've realized, the successes you've achieved, the mistakes you've made, will certainly be appreciated.

The more personality you put in your book, the more it becomes unique. When you write your second book, it will already be sold, because you will already have readers who like your style. In the same way they will want to buy your services, your products, your advice. Because you are YOU, in your uniqueness. So the author's personal brand becomes even more important than the book itself.

The book is a means to let you know and explains the path to deepen your knowledge. It must give the possibility to those who want to grow more, to be able to do it. Otherwise it is a missed opportunity for both you and your reader, who will then turn to someone else.

Do you know how happy and rich my friends and fellow trainers are? When someone reads a book about real estate investments and then writes to our assistance asking "how can I deepen?", We send it to Alfio Bardolla, because he is the number one in that sector. When someone reads a book on motivation, who can he go to? From Roberto Re, who is the number one in his field for twenty years. And so on.

So the book really becomes a formative medium. Imagine you are the reader. Discover a book on a very interesting topic. You like it and you want to put it into practice. You would like to be followed by the author himself, who has demonstrated competence and experience. But find out that he does not sell advice or in-depth products. You are not happy, you are disappointed. And even from the point of view of business it is very wrong for the author.

SECRET n. 29: the focal point is to be consistent with what you teach in your book, so as to build your authority and continue the relationship with the reader.

From a structural point of view, if we think about introduction, contents and conclusion, what is the most important part? If it were the flight of an airplane, the phases would be 3:

Takeoff> Flight> Landing

Let's say that if the plane does not take off, it's definitely a bit 'difficult for it to fly or land. So take off is very important, do you agree?

If I start a book and do not like it, I do not go on reading it, unless it is the school or the university that forces me to do it. And that's why there is a free extract on Amazon, that is the possibility for the reader to have a good experience, that is not to spend money, evaluate it and only later decide whether to buy it or not.

So, for us who want to make sure that our book is ordered, if we want to become the number one in our specific sector, the first part, the flight, the introduction, the free extract, is the most important.

On the Amazon site, there is the "read the extract" function above your cover. It is the first part of the book, 10% offered free to determine if your book will be sold or not and if you become Author Bestseller.

So your focus must be very high on this first part. And it must have a number of features, including that famous summary that you started schematizing on the map. You must create a structured summary according to the "how to" method, because, as I said before, the person can already see all the benefits and results expected from your book. Do not use abstruse, but clear and practical terms, all while providing the right techniques.

Knowing that many will download the extract before buying the book, I explain to the reader that, in the first part, he will find this series of techniques that will allow him to achieve this result, in the second part other techniques, and so on. In this way you have already promoted the book and the desire to continue reading.

Has it ever happened to you, in a novel - maybe a thriller, maybe a thriller, of those very fast and suspenseful - to read the first chapter and look forward to buying it? Because you're in it now, you've become involved in history.

It's like when you go to the movies. You decide whether to see a film or not based on the trailer. Or imagine starting to see a movie and then, after the first half hour, they interrupt you because the projector breaks down. The feeling is of malaise, frustration. When you start, if it's good, you do not want to stop looking at it anymore.

If you like the book, if the book is well written, the first chapter becomes a great tool to make the person want to continue. Because it's normal, start a story, start a journey and do not want it to be interrupted abruptly. Just as when you stop the film you feel an unpleasant sensation, the same happens with the book, because you want to know how it ends. Thus, for all books, including novels, the first part is essential. Start immediately with a quick action.

There are books, especially of known authors, which are very interesting as a case study. For example, in the summer I read a lot and it is the only part of the year when I also read fiction books; a series that I really like is that of Jack Reacher by Lee Child. At the end of each book there is already the entire first chapter of the next book. I start reading, I go into the story and within a few minutes I find myself on Amazon to order the full version of that new book. Generally I read a dozen books in a row, when I start this series.

Maybe it happened to you too. Not with books, but if you have Netflix or similar subscriptions, when you start a TV series it's really hard to stop. I stayed overnight to see 10 series sequential episodes like Prison Break, Narcos or Suits. I do not really love TV, but from these series I learned a lot about how to structure a book. You really never stop learning.

SECRET n. 30: the first part of the book, distributed free of charge, determines if that book will be read and purchased, then take care of it with the utmost care.

In the Amazon extract, which generally corresponds to 10% of the book, all the introduction and most of the first chapter are included. For this reason, already in the first chapter you can give practical strategies, so that your reader can evaluate on his skin and understand that you are good, experienced and able to get him the expected results.

The same concept applies to free writing videos that I distribute for free on YouTube and Facebook. From that information, those who want can already start to throw down a project, to write and understand how to launch their own book. So giving a concrete, valid and valuable example is very positioning.

Another small thing you can do is enter a link to a bonus or extra content. For example, write at the bottom of the introduction "To thank you for downloading my book, I send you 3 training videos on this same topic. Go to www.letturaveloce.net to download them for free ». This link will also see those who download only the extract and the reader will be particularly happy to already be able to access the book's bonuses, even before they have purchased it. For him, a big advantage for you, the possibility of acquiring the customer in your mailing list.

In fact it will arrive on your site, it will leave you the email to access the bonus videos and will enter your list; therefore you will have the opportunity to do the famous marketing and instruct the person on your other products or on your way to work. In this way you will be able to make yourself well known and create a relationship with the reader, which is the most important thing.

When you publish a paper book, even with emblazoned publishers, it ends up in the bookstore and, if you're lucky, also sells copies. But there is no direct relationship, you are not a click away from the reader. It means that the reader must really love you, he must look for you online, he must find you on Facebook, he must ask for friendship and, in any case, he ends up there.

Instead, if you structure the book as I am telling you and publish it on Amazon, your reader is just a click away from you. With a click, the customer accesses your site, where he can leave his email and enter into a relationship with you for weeks, months or years. Do you understand how different, even in this, the digital publishing from the traditional one?

SECRET n. 31: If you structure the book as I am telling you and publish it on Amazon, your reader will be just a click away from you.

So, if the most important part is the take-off, once taken off, even the flight will not be less. The flight is represented by valuable contents, which allow you to increase your authority, to go out of anonymity, to let you know, to position yourself as an expert, to train your readers on what you do and to make them independent of what you have promised them.

The flight represents 80-90% of the book itself. Continue with this copywriting lineup, for each chapter:

- Talk about the goal of the chapter.
- Explain the problem and shake it.
- Anticipate the objections / dispel the myths.
- From value strategies to achieve the goal.
- Tell your story or about other people you've helped.

Here you will go to develop, chapter by chapter, all the contents you have written in your map. Generally for each chapter you will have to develop at least 3 key topics.

As regards the actual writing of the contents, we will discuss it in the next chapter dedicated to the fast writing techniques. For now, the thing to know is that you will have to be very practical.

For my 15 years of experience I can tell you that what people love most is the practice. There is a lot of theory in theory, but the practice represents the work and the actions that people really have to put in place to get a result. So he works in this direction.

SECRET n. 32: Flight is the practical and rich part of your book's contents, in which you can develop your entire topic map.

And the landing? It is however a delicate part. It is where you momentarily close your relationship with the reader and make an invitation to action to continue the relationship.
Then:
- Explain the path to deepen.
- Invite the reader to an action to continue the relationship with you.

Something like this: «Reading this book you have concluded the first step for your growth. If you liked it, go to Amazon and leave me a 5-star review. And, if you want to deepen or want to stay in touch with me, go to my website Mio-Nome.it or Nome-del-libro.it and download the bonus content.

Leave me your email and I will send you newsletters to update you on my work and I will update you on the release of the second volume as soon as it is available».

SECRET n. 33: in the landing insert a contact or registration link to continue the relationship with the reader outside the book.

Then it's up to you, based on the projects you have. Certainly the conclusion has its importance because, if you have written a good book, the reader will want to stay in touch with you, to know what you do, to see if you have kept your promises and so on. Today, that we are all social, it is so easy to keep in touch that it would be a missed opportunity not to keep the relationship alive.

Precisely for this reason I would like to take up the map of your book and try to map, in your project, all the topics to be included in the introduction, in the chapters and in the conclusion. Think about where you want to take your reader once the book is finished. And immediately register the domain name of your book or your name.

Maybe at first you may not realize it but, if you apply the method I'm teaching you, within 3/6 months you'll become number one on Amazon and start having an abundant following of readers and new customers.

SUMMARY OF CHAPTER 4:

- SECRET n. 25: in the structure of your book you can refer to various editing or layout programs, but the best remains Word for simplicity and compatibility.
- SECRET n. 26: evaluate to give your book also free to generate word of mouth, build authoritativeness and create very important automatic income.
- SECRET n. 27: immediately involve your reader by challenging him and telling him about the opportunity he will have in reading your book.
- SECRET n. 28: always provide maximum content and value strategies, so that the reader is completely independent of that topic.
- SECRET n. 29: the focal point is to be consistent with what you teach in your book, so as to build your authority and continue the relationship with the reader.
- SECRET n. 30: the first part of the book, distributed free of charge, determines if that book will be read and purchased, then take care of it with the utmost care.
- SECRET n. 31: If you structure the book as I am telling you and publish it on Amazon, your reader will be just a click away from you.

- SECRET n. 32: Flight is the practical and rich part of your book's contents, in which you can develop your entire topic map.
- SECRET n. 33: in the landing insert a contact or registration link to continue the relationship with the reader outside the book.

Chapter 5:
8 + 2 Speed Writing Techniques

Now we got to a very interesting part; how to write content quickly. I would have paid to know these techniques when, in 2002, I decided to write my first book.

The nice thing for you is that now you take the fruits of my fifteen years of experience. Not by chance, it is this same experience that allowed me to reach 23,000 copies in 24 hours for my penultimate book Marketing Training. And you know what is the most interesting thing? Which in fact I did not even write a page. I know it sounds strange, but if you follow my strategies, you can do it too.

Do you want my secret about how I wrote that book? It's very simple: I picked up my phone, opened a voice recording app, clicked the "REC" button and started recording my voice while explaining marketing concepts. With a few recording sessions, I explained all the concepts, chapter by chapter, with a simple and colloquial language. The same simple language for which my books are so much appreciated and understood by anyone.

This method works because we are all good at talking. And do not tell me you shut up all day because I do not believe it. You can say that you are not technological, that you do not send emails or messages on WhatsApp, or that you do not write often on Facebook, but for sure you speak. In this case you start talking to the cellullare, as if you were making a normal phone call. You can wear the earphones, to be comfortable, and start explaining the topics you've written on the map.

All you need is an app that allows you to record and, if your phone does not have it by default, download one, because there are several, all free. It is very comfortable even when you are not at home or you are not at the computer, maybe you can think of a good idea or an interesting concept to explain, take the phone and register it. You can even speak for five minutes, but those five minutes transcribed become 4/5 pages. And 4 pages today, 5 tomorrow and here in less than a month your book is ready. With an incredible ease.

Once you have registered, you can transfer audio files to your computer and start transcribing them. Or, if you have a friend who takes care of this and can help you to transcribe the audio, for him can mean to scrape some more money and for you an excellent investment.

Or again, you can use the Fiverr.com marketplace where, with a few tens of euros, you can draw on any service. With 50 euros, you can generally write an hour of audio, equal to 50 pages of book. With two hours of audio, you're done and your 100-page book is ready.

So, starting from the map, I recorded one chapter at a time, and in a few hours of work, I was holding a book of over 200 pages. I followed exactly the same instructions that I gave you so far: I created the title, then the map of the project, finally I took my phone and I started to record the contents.

It will come naturally to you, because you are already used to talking. Simply tell and explain things like you would with a friend of yours. Think of how many times you chat with friends and exchange tips, ideas and opinions on anything. At that moment you are forming your friends and they are forming you. They would be pages and pages of books.

Like when your restaurateur friend urges you to go right in his restaurant, and not in others, because he boasts of being the only one to make pasta carbonara in a certain way, with the recipe of the grandmother etc. Or when you describe your business and tell customers what you have unique and special about others. And maybe explain the importance of certain production processes. At that moment you are training, educating, telling your business to someone. It would be the perfect contents for your book.

It also happens when you talk on the phone with a friend and that asks for advice; you describe your strategies, how you would behave and so on. From that conversation could come out an extraordinary book useful to many people. When someone explains something to you, it is forming you, and the transcription would be perfect for making a chapter of a book.

So with your phone, a simple app and 2 total hours of recording, your 100-page book is ready. If we calculate a few hours for the preparatory phase, for the transcripts and for the final revision, it certainly falls within the total 10 hours.

It is the technique I used to write Marketing Training. The book came to over 200 pages because I recorded 4 hours of content. So, if you feel comfortable with this method, nothing prevents you from making further recordings and adding some chapters to make your book more complete, where necessary. Other times, however, 100 pages are more than enough to explain a niche topic and making a longer book would only serve to lengthen the stock, which is not exactly synonymous with quality.

But think about what all this means. In the face of a few hours of work, I created a book that allowed me to make record numbers and get 150,000 euros in the 90 days following the publication. This is NOT a standard result for those who publish a book in Italy. So, once again I tell you that you are in the right place, at the right time, with the right person. Keep following me, and your life will change forever.

On the other hand, in the face of the few hours of work for the realization of the text, we must not forget the 15 years of studies and experiences that I have included in my book. If in a few hours I write a book that after two years is still number one bestseller on Amazon, it is because in the previous 15 years I have deepened and put into practice marketing from morning to night.

So, if the writing process is relatively simple, the content to be shared is not so. For this reason in the first chapters of this book I have insisted so much on the question of finding your uniqueness and your fields of experience. And if you do not have the experience and the expertise, you must acquire them with books, courses and lots of practice.

But if you understand who you are and what you are expert, then, with these techniques and these tools, you are ready to really break through.

SECRET n. 34: the technique n. 1 to write your book even without writing it is to use a voice recording app on your phone and transcribe the contents.

What are the other tools? If you do not have a smartphone, or you simply do not want to record and then transcribe, the second strategy is voice dictation. You know Siri? It is the voice assistant of the iPhone and demonstrates how much speech recognition software has made great strides. In reality, by now, all computers have integrated dictation software. All Macs have voice dictation, but even software such as Office Word has integrated dictation.

I can assure you that they work, because these dictation software I'm trying to use them for fifteen years. I remember the initial versions of Dragon, one of the first speech recognition software. The problem lay in the several hours to be lost in the setup, so that the computer could learn to decipher your voice, the way you were talking. But it never worked very well. The latest versions, however, are great, have evolved a lot.

Even Google has recognition software, now the voice services are normal. When I have to put a destination on the Google Maps navigator, I press the microphone button and speak, without having to type anything. It works perfectly and does not need to be particularly technological.

So, for your book, simply open Word and, if you have one of the latest versions, go to the top menu "Composition"> "Start Dictation". You speak and it writes. If you do not talk excessively fast, the computer follows you well and is really very effective. The advantage, compared to the previous method, is that you do not even have to transcribe, because as you speak, you find the text ready.

On the other hand, you do not have the convenience of always having it at your fingertips like your mobile phone, to pinpoint ideas on the fly. The important thing is that you do not block yourself on the difficulty of writing or not knowing how to use the app or the dictation software, because the opportunity to become a Bestseller author is worth much more. Learn to do what you need, because the world is moving forward and you can not stay behind, you can not stay still.

SECRET n. 35: the technique n. 2 is to use voice dictation software on your computer, so as to speak simply and have the transcription ready.

The third technique is ghostwriting, which is to hire a person to write for you. There are so many famous books that have been written by someone else. You may think that maybe your text could lose personality. But knowing that so many famous authors have used it, I have a duty to list it in this book on writing techniques.

In any case, if you use a ghostwriter, it is not that you then copy-paste his work and the book is ready. You have to put your personality and enrich it with your stories. You always have to give the map, the summary and everything. Do not leave white paper on everything. Give him your cut, the summary, all the work you did and only then can you ask him to write.

I know that many people do not like the ghostwriter's idea. But I also want to tell you something else: maybe you have the idea of the century. Or you simply have life stories to tell that could help millions of people. It would be a shame if they were lost because you do not have the time or the desire to write your book. In this case, rather than giving up, it is better to rely on the ghostwriter, without making too many problems.

Maybe the book loses a bit of personality, but at least the world does not lose your skills. The priority here is always helping others, it's not a writing championship.

SECRET n. 36: the technique n. 3 is to rely on a ghostwriter who can help you write the book and share your knowledge.

At this point, if you think the ghostwriter can be a viable solution, I want to give you another piece of advice. In fact, as an idea I do not like that one writer has your job in hand and that tomorrow, when you become Author Bestseller and sell a million copies, you can boast of having written your book.
So, if you decide to adopt this strategy, do not give everything to one person, but contact 4 or 5 different ghostwriters, to whom you can assign individual chapters or paragraphs in your book.

You may not even reveal to these figures that you are writing a book, but just ask them to help you write articles for your blog; then, by uniting them, a nice chapter can come out and, in the end, a whole book.

SECRET n. 37: the technique n. 4 plans not to entrust your work to a single ghostwriter, but to more people who can write short parts.

You can in fact use these articles for your blog. Written by you or with the help of others, the blog is a great strategy to attract readers. Or to make known your work and your skills. I myself, when in 2002 I started my career in the world of education, I started writing articles in which I shared all the knowledge I had learned from books and applied on myself.

And if you do not have a blog? Start now. Maybe you can start creating it, write one article at a time, calmly, then you shorten them all and create the book. After all, they are nothing but your original contents, they are your ideas.

The first one who is following this strategy is my wife. For a few months he opened his blog on Style Details (www.vivianagrunert.it/en) and, article after article, is having an incredible success. It started from zero and without any push.

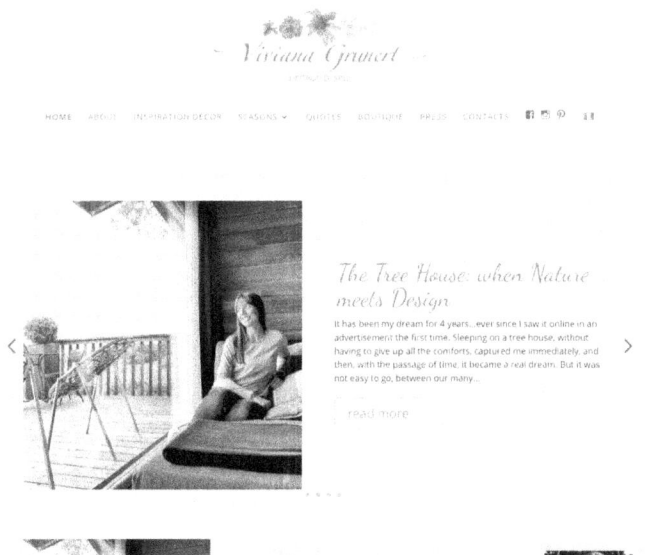

When one day he wants to publish one of his books on this subject, he will already be able to find most of the content ready. Also because each of its educational articles is so long and thorough that it corresponds to 4/5 pages of book. With 20 articles, the book is ready.

In this way it will also have another advantage: it is already beginning to build a following of people. So, when she is ready to launch her book, she will have thousands of downloads from day one and will immediately become bestsellers. A double return of visibility and authority.

Make the mind work, it must be open; you have to make creativity work on all the models you want or want to use to make your book and achieve your purpose.

SECRET n. 38: the technique n. 5 is to write articles for your blog and assemble them in a structured way to create your book.

Now I'm talking about another method that, thanks to my training, I used and use very often. We've seen how to create audio with mobile apps, but now we're working on videos. The method consists of shooting a video and having it written down. You do not even need an expensive technical equipment, since now with the phone you can do all kinds of video, even in Full HD and 4k. It can also become a useful training to explain this technique to someone else. You register as you talk to someone or while you are pretending to do it, and then you write it down with the usual methods we have already seen.

What if I told you that the book you're holding comes from this strategy? Taking care of training for years, I did nothing but shoot 4 hours of video and have them transcribed.

Certainly there is a considerable work of adaptation, because the spoken language is very different from the written one. However, starting with a base of about 180 pages already ready, with all the contents that I had mapped and then recorded, made everything much easier.

Here then explained how I could make this book in a total of less than 10 hours overall:

- 1 hour per title and map design;
- 1 hour for the cover (yes, I did it because I wanted it);
- 4 hours of video recording;
- 3 hours of rehabilitation (6 sessions of 30 minutes);
- ½ hour of final re-reading after proofreading.

TOTAL: 9 HOURS AND HALF

Not bad for a book that, two months before the launch, had already received bookings for thousands of copies and generated a turnover of over 200,000 euros.

Is this a method that is good for everyone? Maybe you never spoke in front of a camera. But given the results, perhaps it would be worth learning. Knowing how to shoot videos is one of those skills that are increasingly valuable in today's social life. Soon Facebook will become the largest video platform in the world, even greater than YouTube, because videos are a type of content that is very viral. It is the new TV for today's young people.

So yes, it's for everyone, and you should spend more time on this project, because it can change your life from every point of view.

SECRET n. 39: the technique n. 6 consists of shooting videos, making them transcribe and then reviewing everything to adapt them to the book.

What if you still do not feel ready to speak in front of a camera? The seventh strategy involves getting interviewed and transcribing the video. Maybe you do not like to stand in front of the camera, or you do not know what to say. But if someone interviews you, asks you the questions and you answer, it's definitely more natural and easier. It can be a good alternative to start.

Be interviewed by a friend, by your partner, by a colleague of your work, by whoever you want, and once you have the filming, you will get a good book on the subject you have to teach. After that you will fix it, you will take care of the editing and you will make your additions, according to the lineup.

SECRET n. 40: the technique n. 7 is to have you interviewed by a friend and shoot everything in video, so as to be able to create a book in a more spontaneous and natural way.

And if you still do not know what to say? The eighth strategy requires you to interview someone, some industry experts, and then transcribe the interviews.

There are books of the highest level that are a collection of interviews; in the United States this method is very popular. For example, you can make a book on entrepreneurship by writing ten interviews of famous Italian entrepreneurs. Would sell a lot, because people are very inspired by the stories of famous people, and you would find yourself with a book of 100/200 pages without having written even one word. Indeed, you would position yourself as someone dealing with entrepreneurs, then influential in turn.

Often these people are more than happy to be interviewed. In general, the entrepreneur can not wait to tell you his story, he loves visibility and knows that you are giving him authority; he spent his soul for his job and the emotions in his story are strong.

I want to bring you the example of The Secret of the Web, the documentary film about the world of web marketing. I am an actor in this film, I was interviewed together with other experts in the marketing and training sector, all authoritative people in their sector, and an extraordinary product came out.

The director had the idea, he directed and edited it, took it all up and pulled out a film with our interviews. Imagine how easy it can be to use all that material to make a book. If he transcribed that documentary, an extraordinary book would come out of it, certainly a bestseller.

SECRET n. 41: the technique n. 8 consists of interviewing experts in your field and creating a very authoritative book with a faithful transcription of all interviews.

Summing up, these are the 8 strategies to create a book without writing it:

1. Voice recording by mobile.
2. Voice dictation on the PC.
3. Relying on a ghostwriter.
4. Delegate short parts to multiple ghostwriters.
5. Assemble blog articles.
6. Video recording.
7. Videointerview to yourself.
8. Video interviews with experts in the sector.

They are all simple strategies to be implemented and within everyone's reach. There are no particular costs, because today with a smartphone you do absolutely everything. And there are not even technical difficulties, so you have no excuse.

If you are more traditional and you like to write, then you can use two strategies. But they are certainly different from traditional techniques, here the writer's block does not exist.

Technique number 9 consists in writing in blocks of 10 minutes, for an average of 500 block words.

If you write 10 minutes a day, you'll get incredible results for a variety of reasons. First of all, the Pareto principle is applied, the one we have seen before, which is valid for the results, for the economy, for a lot of sectors and also for the time, ie 20% of the time gives 80% of the results. So, a small space of time, 10 minutes, at high concentration, will give you great results.

Take the case of a university student; generally, when he has to prepare an exam, he does not do anything for three months and then he reduces himself to studying and applying himself in the last days. Those few days in which he studied, bring 80% of the vote he will take, while the remaining 80% of the time has very little influence. In the same way, you take 10 minutes a day to write your book, but in those 10 focused, write what you really need.

If you do any work and take a 3-hour space, you will realize that 80% of those hours will not be used at all. You lose yourself in another thousand distractions: you sit down, you put yourself in a comfortable position, you decide to reply to emails, open a moment in Facebook, reply to a message on WhatsApp. Moral, the real work, concrete, will last less than half an hour, in which you will have written a few pages. So it's better to decide to dedicate only 10 minutes immediately and focus on the maximum.

This is also confirmed by the Parkinson's law, which states that "work expands to occupy all the available time". If I give you 60 minutes to write 5 pages, you will put exactly 60 of them. You would all use them in some way.

If instead I give you only 10 minutes, you will be precise 10. Not a minute more. When you assign tasks to a person who works with you, if you give him so much time, he will almost certainly take care of everything, regardless of the amount of work.

Exactly how it happens with software: computers continue to increase in memory, power and space, yet it is never enough. The weight of the software itself continues to expand within the computer, you can never be as fast as you would like.

So the result will be that the more time you have, the more you will waste. If you have little time, work more concentrated, for the same reason. When you know that you have to meet a deadline and you have only tomorrow to complete a project, you firmly decide to finish it, even at midnight, one or two at night, but you complete it, because you know you have a compressed time and use it to the maximum of your strength.

If you have too much time, time expands; if you have little time, you work well.

So the invitation I give you is to dedicate 10 minutes a day, because in those 10 minutes you will complete your book. At this point, set a tight deadline and I guarantee you that with 10 minutes a day you will write your book, much more likely than you would have if I gave you 3 months to write it.

Do you think 10 minutes are a few? I show you what you can do in 10 minutes. Consider that a short email is around 250 words. I just counted them, an email in which I replied to a friend giving him some information; they were a couple of paragraphs, but very short, a few lines each. A medium-length email reaches 500 words, which is already a very good level.

The emails I used in communications to launch this book were a little longer, because I told my stories, my travels, my adventures, and they were around 750 words. Let's take a middle course, consider writing an average 500-word email, which is our goal.

As I have already pointed out in the introduction of this book, 500 words a day for 30 days are 15,000 words which, in turn, are 100 pages. So you will have made your book in 30 days, if you have decided to apply even those 10 minutes a day. Which is equivalent to a total of 300 minutes, 5 work hours.

There will be no circumstances that can prevent you from finding those 10 minutes a day. Maybe you can find them in the first part of the morning. In one of the best-selling bestsellers of the moment, The Miracle Morning, the author explains how to manage the routines of the morning to leave with great energy and also to find 10 minutes a day to write. When this book arrived in Italy it became one of the top bestsellers, with tens of thousands of copies sold. It tells you that if you wake up early in the morning, apart from the first five minutes that are the most difficult to overcome, you can earn an hour or more a day, and at that time, you can spend 10 minutes doing the healthy exercise physical, 10 more to write and 10 more to the things that make you feel good. And so on. These are the habits that change your life.

Doing it in the morning is just an idea, but you can do it in the evening, maybe someone is much more productive at this time of day. But it is important that you do not burn any day, because if you lose even one day, skip the attitude. From there begins a series of excuses, which lead to postpone the work and think that the next day you can do it for twenty minutes. The next day you realize that you have no desire to work, those twenty minutes become thirty and goodbye book.

So, if you decide to apply this technique, take the commitment to carry it forward. It's only 10 minutes a day, and it's only 30 days of effort. You can do it.

SECRET n. 42: the technique n. 9 is to make a commitment to write 10 minutes a day for 30 days, so in a month you will have already completed your book.

It's not over. I still have a technique and that's exactly what I'm using as I write these lines. Right now I'm in Ibiza, I'm re-editing the transcripts of my videos and I'm adding some parts, including this one.

Here life does not take place according to my daily routine. I'm on vacation and I do not have an office where I can go to work in peace. Nor is it particularly easy to wake up in the morning when you are late in the evening. So skip to me the 10-minute routine in the morning too.

Having estimated in about 3 hours the work necessary to complete this book, I decided to dedicate 6 sessions of 30 minutes to writing. If you think about it, the concept is the same as before: to establish a specific, short, very limited space of time in which to focus on concentration at work.

So after being at the beach, back home, I take a shower and from 19.00 to 19.30 literally disappears. I turn off the phone, I ask the family not to be disturbed and I lock myself in my room or by the pool with my MacBook Air. Cascass the world, in those 30 minutes I carry on my work, exactly as I planned it.

And so it was. Now that I am rereading the final version of the book, I can confirm that I have complied with the exact times and, in 3 hours total, I have completed the revision of the book. So, if you think that 10 minutes a day is too distracting in your daily routine to keep for at least 30 days, you can reduce the commitment to fewer days, as long as you can cut out the duration blocks of time greater in which you are hyperconcentrated.

Does this mean that if you really concentrate you could do the 10 hours of work all in one day? I would say no, it would really be alienating. However you can push yourself to a block of an hour. Over this time, you risk falling into the various laws of Pareto and Parkinson's and going to create excessive waste of time for lack of real concentration.

SECRET n. 43: the technique n. 10 plans to carve blocks of 30/60 minutes for a smaller number of days, so as to remain focused and be even faster in making the book.

At this point, with blocks for an hour, it would be to engage for only 10 days. On the other hand, the level of concentration required is higher than the daily 10 minutes.

But as much as the effort can be raised at the mental level, remember that, on the other hand, the result will last for a lifetime.

SUMMARY OF CHAPTER 5:

- SECRET n. 34: the technique n. 1 to write your book even without writing it is to use a voice recording app on your phone and transcribe the contents.
- SECRET n. 35: the technique n. 2 is to use voice dictation software on your computer, so as to speak simply and have the transcription ready.
- SECRET n. 36: the technique n. 3 is to rely on a ghostwriter who can help you write the book and share your knowledge.
- SECRET n. 37: the technique n. 4 plans not to entrust your work to a single ghostwriter, but to more people who can write short parts.
- SECRET n. 38: the technique n. 5 is to write articles for your blog and assemble them in a structured way to create your book.
- SECRET n. 39: the technique n. 6 consists of shooting videos, making them transcribe and then reviewing everything to adapt them to the book.
- SECRET n. 40: the technique n. 7 is to have you interviewed by a friend and shoot everything in video, so as to be able to create a book in a more spontaneous and natural way.
- SECRET n. 41: the technique n. 8 consists of interviewing experts in your field and creating a very authoritative book with a faithful transcription of all interviews.
- SECRET n. 42: the technique n. 9 is to make a commitment to write 10 minutes a day for 30 days, so in a month you will have already completed your book.

- SECRET n. 43: the technique n. 10 plans to carve blocks of 30/60 minutes for a smaller number of days, so as to remain focused and be even faster in making the book.

Conclusion

"Number 1 does not mean being perfect. It means being the best version of yourself."

I wanted to write this book to help you become a real Bestseller Author number one on Amazon and, in general, number one in life.

So, if you have understood what my mission is in life, you will have already realized that the book is only the first stone, the first brick.

When I read Anthony Robbins' book, I had enlightenment, but then I worked hard and I read another 700 books in a year, I attended courses and I changed my life.

In practice I started a journey.
That has lasted for over 15 years.

For this reason I would like you to start a path of personal and professional growth. In Italy, besides me, there are many training professionals with whom you can start a journey and, if you need advice, you can always write me on Facebook and I will be happy to help you.

Personally I created the path I wanted to have for myself 15 years ago. It's called **Numero1** ™ and is a live event, with 1,000 participants, where we go to work together to carry out the book and become Author Bestseller.

So far you've seen the design and writing part. But there are 3 other steps that are absolutely essential:
- How to publish your book, with a publisher or in self-publishing.
- How to launch it on the market and become Amazon bestseller.
- How to monetize your book and create automatic income.

You will have noticed in these pages, how important is the part of marketing to promote your book and launch it effectively. It would really be a waste if, after all the work you are doing now to create your first book, then this is not properly launched on the market. You can not afford it. I want your knowledge to reach thousands of people. On the course days in the classroom, we will start from scratch to develop your book and make sure that it becomes, with absolute certainty, a bestseller. Because you will learn to master the Amazon search engine and I will give you the exact strategies to be first with your book. And again, I'll talk to you about business. Because maybe you're writing a book to help people and bring value to the market. And when you work well, you have an important economic return.

At Numero1 ™ you will have learned how to design, starting from your book, a business that can bring you very high income.

If you think about the book *Training Marketing*, given as a tribute to Amazon, took me over 3 months over 150,000 euros. This same book you have in your hand, *3X Speed Writing*, even two months before the launch had already received bookings for thousands of copies and generated a turnover of over 200,000 euros.

You will get this kind of return if you respect 3 golden rules:
- Write a book that can bring great value to the market, with tips and practical strategies.
- Connect your book to a well-designed launch system to become Amazon bestsellers.
- Being able to reach thousands of people through Facebook strategies.

This is why in recent years we have invested over € 500,000 for the 3 magic ingredients that I provide and teach during the course:

BookMap ™ - A unique way to design your book in less than 60 minutes. It is the result of 15 years of work on over 600 published books.

AmzRank1 ™ - The secret algorithm to climb Amazon's bestseller rankings in just 6 hours since the launch of your book. An exclusive of Numero1 ™.

LeadFace ™ - The training marketing system to create customers via Facebook for your book and / or your business.

Numero1 ™ has been defined the number one course in Europe to become Bestseller Author. Because with Bruno Editore, in these 15 years of experience, unlike traditional publishers who often publish you in exchange for money and do not advertise you, we specialize in marketing and book promotion. This means that we know exactly how to make you become Bestseller Author on Amazon.

You can think that for me, after 15 years, it's easier. But actually, if you have strategies in hand, it's easy for you too. Let me introduce you to the people who participated in the previous edition of the course.

"I came with a little skepticism about writing a book, but I participated enthusiastically in the course. I followed all the recommended steps to the letter and, after a short time from the course, in less than 24 hours, I became bestseller on Amazon with over 2,000 copies. The promise has been more than kept."

Piernando Binaghi

«I wrote my top Physical book in just 5 days and became a bestseller in less than an hour. I did not think I could reach these goals. The publisher's promise has been widely maintained. I applied the steps, I put the right effort and the m. the skills and everything else was done by the publisher. Becoming a Bestseller Author is possible. I recommend  the Numero1 ™ course because it is practical, effective and reliable. Being guided and accompanied by professionals is essential for becoming a number one in your field.»

Veronica Tudor

"Before I joined Number1 ™, I had written another book. Time to finish it: 2 years. Copies sold: only to friends and acquaintances. Then I took part in Numero1 ™ and, with the precious advice I learned during the course, I not only wrote the book in a very short time, but in less  than 3 months I was already a Bestseller Author. What about ... Giacomo Bruno guarantee of success!»

Carmen Debora Esposito

"I had come to the course out of pure curiosity. I came out with great inspiration and, in less than 60 days, I wrote my book, Changing the Past, from scratch. At the time of the launch, in a few hours I became bestseller n. 1 on Amazon and I received dozens of super positive comments from people to whom I could change my life. Very happy!"

Rubina Guacci

"As a business coach and mental trainer, writing a coaching book was essential to help many more people develop their potential. By attending Numero1 ™ I published the book, immediately becoming bestsellers and reaching many more customers for coaching and training courses.»

Alex Abate

«Giacomo struck me both for his disarming enthusiasm and for his great professionalism. I wrote a scientific manual related to my work in just 3 months. An absolute record, a 20-year project realized in such a short time. Thanks to the information and knowledge learned during

the course, I decided to make the book become a mission for me and to change people's lives."

Velia Tortora

"I always had the dream of writing a book even if I did not even know the subject. Thanks to Numero1 ™ I not only discovered the most suitable theme for my experiences and passions, but I designed, with a disarming simplicity, every single chapter of the book. The visualization of why to write it was the fuel that fueled the dream that is finally being realized. »

Massimo Minoletti

"I was tired and depressed, with a seasonal job. I found myself at 50 years of not knowing more than what direction to take. I was looking, but I did not know what. Only an intense desire to change. I attended the course to spend a different weekend and I found there the turning point I was looking for. Thanks to the course I can put to good use years of experience and hard work. I like the idea of helping others make their dreams come true. "

Alessandra Di Napoli

«Numero1 ™ was a real springboard to success for me. Before attending the course, I had only the idea of wanting to write a book. I had the title and some notes. Three months later, instead, I found myself Author Bestseller in first place in the Amazon ranking. Extraordinary. Thank you!"

Roberto Martufi

"Publishing a book has been one of my dreams since I was a child. I have always written a lot but I have never yet published a book. I attended the Numero1 ™ course which gave me all the tools to write, publish and make a book bestseller. The course is really useful, well structured and accessible to everyone. I decided to write a book about my business change management activity: [R] -Company Evolution, which helps entrepreneurs, managers, professionals and collaborators to evolve themselves and the company from a mental, strategic and organizational point of view. The book has become the bestseller most downloaded in Italy and often in its specific ranking is among the most purchased. Without the Numero1 ™ course this important result would never have been possible. "

Andrea Rubes Albinati

"I took part in the Numero1 ™ course with the desire to write a book, but thinking I would not be able to do it. I went out with all the necessary tools to start writing my first book: Melt your body. Now I've become no.1 bestseller on Amazon and my life is changing. Great satisfaction and growth! "

Gloria Spiritelli

"I did not think of writing a book. As in the dream book it was something that I imagined was too difficult for me. While I listened to the steps indicated by Giacomo, everything seemed terribly simpler, to the point of thinking of making it. So I left the classroom with the title Smart Company and with the titles of the chapters of what would become my bestseller. Today is my pride and my most powerful marketing tool. "

Ernesto Petricca

"Mine was a conscious choice because I already knew Giacomo and I knew he would keep his commitments. I followed his advice to the course and, in addition to my book, my wife's novel became a bestseller Amazon. Incredible but true. "

Angelo Emidio Lupo

«One day on Facebook I listen to Giacomo who in a clear and clear way says that one can write a book. I'm skeptical but I want to do it. So I enrolled in the course and I find people who, like me, want to do something to improve their lives and that of others. On the first day of the course I write the title of the book Swimming without water and in four months, despite my very demanding work, I finish it. Once published, he immediately became a bestseller. To date for my category, in Rome, I am the first author. Thank you."

Patrizia Silberheer

"I've always had in mind to write a book. The biggest obstacle I thought was not only how to write it, but above all how to publish it. Thanks to Numero1 ™ by Giacomo Bruno and his editorial group, all my qualms have been overcome. If only six months ago I had tried to imagine what was waiting for me, my most optimistic forecasts would not have hit the mark. Today, in a short time I wrote the book, it was published, I became the author Bestseller, I gave new impetus to my profession and I was invited to give lectures on the subject of the book in University Masters. What to expect more? "

Giancarlo Paga

"At least twenty years ago I had the idea of writing a book. I also tried, some draft, some pages ... but I have always stranded! Then I saw a message on Facebook and I signed up for the course. I was not even sure to participate. Today, after only six months, thanks to the path of Numero1 ™, I wrote, published and achieved the result of Author Bestseller. I am writing two more books that I will publish later this year. Incredible! "

Piergiorgio Franchini

«I've had an electrocution, one of those moments when suddenly a crazy idea materializes in my mind, something I had never thought of before. And so, by pure chance I participated in the Event (and the capital letter is not used randomly) Numero1 ™. Of course I was skeptical, but basically I  wanted with all my strength that someone could deny me. I a writer and even bestseller? Impossible. And then, as the hours passed in the courtroom with Giacomo, every skepticism was shattered, every doubt dispelled.»

Mauro Imparato

"Do I write a book? Maybe. But I do not think I can. Thinking about the title I would have it: The Comprocasa Method. Ok I'll try. After 5 months I complete the writing of my book, hopefully well. The public and ... The Comprocasa Method is bestseller on Amazon! It was enough to trust and follow the instructions. When a publisher's  goal is to take care of their authors, then you understand that you're in the right place at the right time. Then, with the right commitment, it will be inevitable to understand that you are also the right person. "

Luigi Ilardi

"I have heard many times: You will write a book! Then I also received a proposal from a friend of mine who follows a series of books from a classic publishing house. But I did not feel ready. Thanks to the Numero1 ™ course I realized that I do not write the book just for myself, but also to help others. I probably  would have written the book anyway but, thanks to the Numero1 ™ course, I anticipated at least 10 years. Thank you, Giacomo Bruno! "

Mihail Bria

"I was thinking for some time to write for my patients a book that contained the advice I gave during visits. The excuses were many: I do not have time, I do not know who to turn to, as I write ... And so I had always postponed. Then the moment arrived: I enrolled in the Numero1 ™ course and an  unforgettable experience began that continues today. I wrote my book Fear of the dentist, goodbye, I published it, I became a bestseller author, I got recognition from colleagues, patients and, above all, I am aware of having helped raise the consciousness of many who thought they could never do.

You can and must always, the monsters of fear can be destroyed once and for all. If you keep your focus on fire you will always reach it. "
Laura Vedani

«A few years ago I started interviewing some clients who underwent reiki, ayurveda, reflexology, floristry and other holistic methods that I conceived and taught to the beautician colleagues, received a series of benefits, and excited by their joy I had decided while taking notes. Then I attended the Numero1 ™ event and I followed the instructions of Giacomo Bruno. What I wrote during those days! Something clicked in me that spurred me to choose to concentrate and do it. For once I let perfectionism go. Just among some phrases of Giacomo there is that if your fear of writing a book is grammar, then let your talent flow: essential is not the form but the value of the content! »

Tiziana Gargiulo

***

For me it was an honor to accompany these people to their goal and if there is one thing I really care about is keeping promises. If I say one thing it's that, and I really believe that the Numero1 ™ course is the first course in Italy with 100% satisfied people and 100% results. Yes, 100%

of the authors that we published after the course have become Authors Bestseller number 1 on Amazon. All.

I'm not saying it's simple. I'm saying that if you get busy and follow the instructions I gave you in this book, then your destiny will magically also lead you to become Bestseller Author. And that while you're helping your readers improve their lives. This makes everything really magical.

So, if you want to start this journey, made of a bit of magic and dreams that come true, here you find all the information to change your life and become number one:

www.brunoeditore.it

I'll wait for you!
Giacomo Bruno

Do you want to publish your book with Bruno Editore?

We receive an average of 3 proposals a day. They are 1,000 in a year. And we only have 52 seats every year. Since we have chosen to publish only Bestseller books, the selection is tight and accurate.

Publishing with Bruno Editore means having immediate authority, enormous visibility and GUARANTEE to become a Bestseller in 24 hours. Over 600 Authors have already published with Bruno Editore from 2002 to today.

Each publication costs us thousands of euros between editorial work and advertising costs, so we look for authors who have invested time and money on their project and their training. Because the author must be the first to believe in his book and invest in himself. The Bruno Editore team is waiting for you!

www.brunoeditore.it

www.ingramcontent.com/pod-product-compliance
Lightning Source LLC
Chambersburg PA
CBHW070807230426
43665CB00017B/2522